ISBN 9781980283805

Contents

Dedications:

This book is dedicated to two extraordinary individuals.

First, to my wife Sheryl. She has been there for me, in good times and bad, throughout our marriage of over four years. She also helped to edit this book. Happy belated anniversary, my love.

Second, to my mother, Susan Peterson. What can I say? You believed in me and pushed me to trust myself every step of the way. You also helped in the editing process. This book wouldn't have been possible without you.

Author Biography: Matthew S. Thomas, Esquire

Matthew Thomas is an attorney and political scientist. He humbly begs that neither of these be held against him.

When not reading or writing a book, Matthew writes articles for The Upbeat Conservative website, practices law, and works on plans for a soon-to-open YouTube channel. He is also fluent in Spanish.

Matthew's hobbies include Olympic and Viking-style fencing (sword fighting), American History, and spending time with his wife and family in beautiful Erie, PA.

Please follow The Upbeat Conservative and the on social media at https://www.facebook.com/The-Upbeat-Conservative-122526687933491 and https://twitter.com/upbeatconserv. If you want to financially support our mission to continue publishing conservative content, you can do so by going to https://www.patreon.com/UConservative and making a donation.

Cover Design by Whitney Leckenby

Whitney Leckenby is a brilliant young graphic designer from Lacey, Washington. A devoted Catholic (and devoted owner of pomeranian pooches) Whitney enjoys spending time with her many brothers, sisters, cousins, and friends.

Whitney also suffers from a rare connective tissue disease known as Fibrodysplasia ossificans progressiva, or FOP. This disease causes muscle and other soft tissue in the body to turn to bone, especially when injured (or when surgery is attempted to remove the excess bone). Recent developments in FOP research and in clinical drug tests on human patients have led to significant progress in slowing unwanted bone-growth, and it is hoped that the Food and Drug Administration will soon give full approval for these new treatments. However, a cure for the disease is still badly needed. To learn more, or to donate to FOP research efforts, visit www.ifopa.org.

FOP research involves a rather tight-knit community and group of professionals, and the reader can have confidence that their money will be put to good use.

Proof that America's Founding Fathers were Conservative

493 Quotes for Conservatives, Republicans, Libertarians, and Tea Partiers from America's Founding Fathers

With John Locke and Alexis de Toqueville

Introduction

In our time, the words of America's founding fathers represent many things – not in the least, political currency. With the freedom brought on by the internet, every American now has the ability to not only research, but to join the debate formerly waged primarily by political parties.

Among America's Founders, names like George Washington, Thomas Jefferson, John Adams, Benjamin Franklin, Samuel Adams, Thomas Paine, and Benjamin Rush loom large. Regarding the thoughts and writings of these seven, plus enlightenment philosopher John Locke, from whom they took many of their ideas, and Alexis de Tocqueville, the man who wrote the most seminal study of political science ever to examine the American condition, this work will settle the debate between liberals and conservatives once and for all.

All of the Founders in this book had what we would now call conservative ideas (as did John Locke). In their time, these ideas (such as limited government) were referred to as liberal. Toqueville's early 1830s observations on the America the founders bequeathed to their children confirm their "conservative" ideas again and again, until they are beyond question.

If liberals and Democrats wish to continue advocating their ideology, they must no longer look to the Founding Fathers for support.

How to Read This Book

This book is organized to make it easy for both casual readers and scholars to be able to find what they want, find it quickly, and have a citation for it right in front of them. Thus, each of the nine individuals quoted in this book has their own chapter, and within each chapter, their quotes are broken down by topic. The citation for the quote's source material is then provided in a numbered footnote at the bottom of the same page, so you will immediately know where the quote came from. In addition, each piece of source material is fully cited in a "Works Cited" section at the end.

Samuel Adams, Quotes for Conservatives and Republicans

The importance of Samuel Adams to the American republic is hard to overstate.

One of the colonies' most prolific and liberty-minded authors, he was among the first to call for resistance against the British parliament's attempts to levy taxes on the American colonies.

Displaying a genius for debate, he was probably the first prominent individual to argue that, by previous royal charter, parliament had no authority over the colonies, a point he made in numerous published articles. The royal charters establishing each colony, he argued, gave *limited* governing authority to the king – and only to the king. Thus, Adams provided the basic legal justification for the American refusal to obey tax laws – and eventually for revolution.

A decade later, the resistance that Adams helped spark – and was still helping to trigger – would turn into the Revolutionary War. As had been the case in the past, Adams was closely involved in the action.

Along with other leaders in Boston, Adams likely helped plan (and certainly made political use of) the Boston Tea Party– a destruction of hundreds of chests of tea that had arrived in Boston by ship, and upon which the British parliament had levied a tax. The American colonists had been given no say in the enactment of that tax, and the destruction of the tea was carried out make sure that no one would pay it.

Outraged, the British government ordered their military forces to occupy the city, and to seize colonial stores of weapons nearby. That set off a chain of events that led to a battle in nearby Lexington – in fact, a key reason that Lexington became a British target was that Samuel Adams was hiding there, along with fellow patriot John Hancock.

The ensuing battles of Lexington and nearby Concord placed any real hope of reconciliation between the colonies and Britain beyond reach. Although the colonies had yet to declare themselves independent, America's revolution really began there. Adams and Hancock escaped, and the war was on.

Along with fifty-four other elected leaders from the thirteen colonies, Samuel Adams would go on to sign the Declaration of Independence, just above the signature of his cousin, John Adams, whose ideas will be quoted later in this book.

Here are Samuel Adams' thoughts and words, which agree closely with modern conservative and Republican principles.

On Limited Government:

"They [the legislature] ought to consider the fundamental [constitutional] laws as sacred, if the nation has not in very express terms, given them the power to change them."[1] - Samuel Adams

---

[1] Samuel Adams "Letter to the Governor, 1773" in The Writings of Samuel Adams Volume II, ed. Harry Alonso

"Some of our Politicians would have the People believe that Administration are disposed or determined to have all the Grievances which we complain of redressed, if we will only be quiet."[2] - Samuel Adams

"When an act injurious to freedom has once been done, and the people bear it, the repetition of it is more likely to meet with submission."[3] - Samuel Adams

"It is a pitiful constitution indeed, which so far from being fixed and permanent as it should be - sacred and unalterable in the hands of those where the community has placed it, depends entirely upon the breath of a minister [of state], or of any man..." [4] - Samuel Adams

"The People here are indeed greatly tenacious of their just Rights & I hope in God they will ever firmly maintain them." [5] - Samuel Adams

"It is enough for those who are dependent upon the great for commissions, pensions, and the like, to preach up implicit faith in the great - Others whose minds are unfettered will think for themselves..." [6] - Samuel Adams

"Every wise governor will relinquish a power which is not clearly constitutional..." [7] - Samuel Adams

"PERHAPS there never was a people who discovered themselves more strongly attached to their natural and constitutional rights and liberties, than the British Colonists on this American Continent." [8] - Samuel Adams

"We seem, Messrs. Printers, to be drawing very near the time, when some people will be hardy enough to dispute, whether we are to be governed according to the rule of the Constitution, the building of which has been the Work of Ages, or to use the words of the House, by the "breath of a Minister of State." [9] - Samuel Adams

---

Cushing (Amazon Kindle), Kindle Location 92 percent of 100.

[2] Samuel Adams "Letter to Joseph Hawley, 1773" in The Writings of Samuel Adams Volume III, ed. Harry Alonso Cushing (Amazon Kindle), Kindle Location 16 percent of 100.

[3] Samuel Adams "Candidus, 1771" in The Writings of Samuel Adams Volume II, ed. Harry Alonso Cushing (Amazon Kindle), Kindle Location 63 percent of 100.

[4] Samuel Adams "Candidus, 1771" in The Writings of Samuel Adams Volume II, ed. Harry Alonso Cushing (Amazon Kindle), Kindle Location 50 percent of 100.

[5] Samuel Adams "Letter to Stephen Sayre, 1770" in The Writings of Samuel Adams Volume II, ed. Harry Alonso Cushing (Amazon Kindle), Kindle Location 13 percent of 100.

[6] Samuel Adams "A Chatterer, 1770" in The Writings of Samuel Adams Volume II, ed. Harry Alonso Cushing (Amazon Kindle), Kindle Location 10 percent of 100.

[7] Samuel Adams "Candidus, 1771" in The Writings of Samuel Adams Volume II, ed. Harry Alonso Cushing (Amazon Kindle), Kindle Location 64 percent of 100.

[8] Samuel Adams "Candidus, 1771" in The Writings of Samuel Adams Volume II, ed. Harry Alonso Cushing (Amazon Kindle), Kindle Location 45 percent of 100.

[9] Samuel Adams "A Chatterer, 1770" in The Writings of Samuel Adams Volume II, ed. Harry Alonso Cushing (Amazon Kindle), Kindle Location 9 percent of 100.

"The fears and jealousies of the people are not always groundless: And when they become general, it is not to be presum'd that they are; for the people in general seldom complain, without some good reason." [10] - Samuel Adams

"But the true patriot, will constantly be jealous of those very [governing] men: Knowing that power, especially in times of corruption, makes men wanton; that it intoxicates the mind; and unless those with whom it is entrusted, are carefully watched, such is the weakness or the preverseness of human nature, they will be apt to domineer over the people, instead of governing them, according to the known laws of the state, to which alone they have submitted." [11] - Samuel Adams

"Gladly would some, even of the Clergy, persuade this people to be at ease; and for the sake of peace...to acquiesce in unconstitutional revenue acts, arbitrary ministerial mandates, and absolute despotic independent governors, &c. &c." [12] - Samuel Adams

"And shall we easily be persuaded to take it for granted that such men are incapable of abusing the high trust reposed in them..." [13] - Samuel Adams

"...The necessity and importance of a legislative in being, and of its having the opportunity of exerting itself upon all proper occasions, must be obvious to a man of common discernment."[14] - Samuel Adams

"It is impolitick to make the first attempt to enslave mankind by force: This strikes the imagination, and is alarming: "Important changes insensibly happen: It is against silent & slow attacks that a nation ought to be particularly on its guard.""[15] - Samuel Adams

"...the nation will at length revert to justice. But before that time comes, it is to be feared they will be so accustomed to bondage, as to forget they were ever free." [16] - Samuel Adams

"For I have truly no property in that, which another can by right take from me when he pleases, against my consent." [17] - Samuel Adams

"We cannot think the doctrine of the right of Parliament to tax us is given up, while an act remains in force for that purpose...and the longer it remains the more danger there is of the people's becoming so accustomed to arbitrary and unconstitutional taxes, as to pay them

---

[10] Samuel Adams "Vindex, 1771" in The Writings of Samuel Adams Volume II, ed. Harry Alonso Cushing (Amazon Kindle), Kindle Location 33 percent of 100.

[11] Ibid.

[12] Samuel Adams "Candidus, 1771" in The Writings of Samuel Adams Volume II, ed. Harry Alonso Cushing (Amazon Kindle), Kindle Location 39 percent of 100.

[13] Samuel Adams "A Chatterer, 1770" in The Writings of Samuel Adams Volume II, ed. Harry Alonso Cushing (Amazon Kindle), Kindle Location 10 percent of 100.

[14] Samuel Adams "Vindex, 1770" in The Writings of Samuel Adams Volume II, ed. Harry Alonso Cushing (Amazon Kindle), Kindle Location 1 percent of 100.

[15] Samuel Adams "Vindex, 1771" in The Writings of Samuel Adams Volume II, ed. Harry Alonso Cushing (Amazon Kindle), Kindle Location 34 percent of 100.

[16] Samuel Adams "Letter to Arthur Lee, 1771" in The Writings of Samuel Adams Volume II, ed. Harry Alonso Cushing (Amazon Kindle), Kindle Location 42 percent of 100.

[17] Samuel Adams "Candidus, 1771" in The Writings of Samuel Adams Volume II, ed. Harry Alonso Cushing (Amazon Kindle), Kindle Location 46 percent of 100.

without discontent; and then, as you justly observe, no Minister will ever think of taking them off, but will rather be encouraged to add others."[18] - Samuel Adams

"Every one sees the necessity of this to preserve the balance of power and the freedom of any state: A power without a check, is subversive of all freedom..."[19] - Samuel Adams

"...No Character appears with a stronger Luster in my Mind, than that of a Man, who nobly perseveres in the Cause of publick Liberty, and Virtue..."[20] - Samuel Adams

"...Principiis obstra [resist the first advances] is a maxim worth regarding in politics as well as morals, and it is more especially to be observed, when those who are the most assiduous in their endeavours to alter the civil Constitution, are not less so in persuading us to go to sleep and dream that we are in a state of perfect security."[21] - Samuel Adams

"Had the Body of this People shown a proper Resentment, at the time when the proud Taskmasters first made their appearance, we should never have seen Pensioners multiplying like the Locusts in Egypt, which devoured every green Thing."[22] - Samuel Adams

"The truth is, every man in power will be adulated by some sort of men in every country, because he is a man in power..."[23] - Samuel Adams

"Kings and Governors may be guilty of treason and rebellion: And they have in general in all ages and countries been more frequently guilty of it, than their subjects."[24] - Samuel Adams

"Great pains we know are taken perswade and assure us, that as long as we continue quiet, nothing will be done to our prejudice: But let us beware of these soothing arts. - Has anything been done for our relief? - Has any one grievance which we have complained of been redressed?"[25] - Samuel Adams

"If therefore the preservation of property is the very end of government, we are depriv'd of that for which government itself is instituted."[26] - Samuel Adams

---

[18] Samuel Adams "The House of Representatives of Massachusetts to Benjamin Franklin, 1771" in The Writings of Samuel Adams Volume II, ed. Harry Alonso Cushing (Amazon Kindle), Kindle Location 39 percent of 100.

[19] Samuel Adams "The House of Representatives of Massachusetts to Benjamin Franklin, 1771" in The Writings of Samuel Adams Volume II, ed. Harry Alonso Cushing (Amazon Kindle), Kindle Location 40 percent of 100.

[20] Samuel Adams "Letter to John Wilkes, 1770" in The Writings of Samuel Adams Volume II, ed. Harry Alonso Cushing (Amazon Kindle), Kindle Location 23 percent of 100.

[21] Samuel Adams "Candidus, 1771" in The Writings of Samuel Adams Volume II, ed. Harry Alonso Cushing (Amazon Kindle), Kindle Location 50 percent of 100.

[22] Samuel Adams "Valerius Poplicola, 1772" in The Writings of Samuel Adams Volume II, ed. Harry Alonso Cushing (Amazon Kindle), Kindle Location 73 percent of 100.

[23] Samuel Adams "Candidus, 1771" in The Writings of Samuel Adams Volume II, ed. Harry Alonso Cushing (Amazon Kindle), Kindle Location 43 percent of 100.

[24] Samuel Adams "Candidus, 1771" in The Writings of Samuel Adams Volume II, ed. Harry Alonso Cushing (Amazon Kindle), Kindle Location 59 percent of 100.

[25] Samuel Adams "Candidus, 1771" in The Writings of Samuel Adams Volume II, ed. Harry Alonso Cushing (Amazon Kindle), Kindle Location 54 percent of 100.

[26] Samuel Adams "Candidus, 1771" in The Writings of Samuel Adams Volume II, ed. Harry Alonso Cushing (Amazon Kindle), Kindle Location 65 percent of 100.

"Tyrants alone, says the great Vatel, will treat as seditious, those brave and resolute citizens, who exhort the people to preserve themselves from oppression, in vindication of their rights and privileges..."[27] - Samuel Adams

"If men through fear, fraud or mistake, should in terms renounce and give up any essential natural right, the eternal law of reason and the great end of society, would absolutely vacate such renunciation; the right to freedom being the gift of God Almighty, it is not in the power of Man to alienate this gift, and voluntarily become a slave..."[28] - Samuel Adams

"For my own Part, I pay very little Regard to Addresses to Great Men: Whenever they appear to be but the Breath of Flattery, they must be offensive to the Ears of any Man who has the Feelings of Truth and Sincerity in his own Breast."[29] - Samuel Adams

"The fear of the Peoples abusing their Liberty is made an Argument against their having the Enjoyment of it; as if any thing were so much to be dreaded by Mankind as Slavery."[30] - Samuel Adams

"We are perswaded that the Town whom we have the Honor to serve...have nothing in view but to assist in "endeavoring to preserve our happy civil Constitution free from Innovation & maintain it inviolate"..."[31] - Samuel Adams

"They were certainly misrepresented in the most shameful Manner, when, in order to enslave them it was suggested that they were too ignorant to enjoy Liberty."[32] - Samuel Adams

"The people of this Province, behold with indignation a lawless army posted in its capital, with a professed design to overturn their free constitution."[33] - Samuel Adams

"If they would not pull down kings, let them not support tyrants..."[34] - Samuel Adams

On Morality, Religion and Government:

---

[27] Samuel Adams "Candidus, 1772" in The Writings of Samuel Adams Volume II, ed. Harry Alonso Cushing (Amazon Kindle), Kindle Location 70 percent of 100.

[28] Samuel Adams "The Rights of The Colonists, a List of Violations of Rights and a Letter of Correspondence, 1772" in The Writings of Samuel Adams Volume II, ed. Harry Alonso Cushing (Amazon Kindle), Kindle Location 76 percent of 100.

[29] Samuel Adams "Candidus, 1771" in The Writings of Samuel Adams Volume II, ed. Harry Alonso Cushing (Amazon Kindle), Kindle Location 39 percent of 100.

[30] Samuel Adams "Letter to James Warren, 1775" in The Writings of Samuel Adams Volume III, ed. Harry Alonso Cushing (Amazon Kindle), Kindle Location 60 percent of 100.

[31] Samuel Adams "The Committee of Correspondence of Boston to the Committee of Littleton, 1773" in The Writings of Samuel Adams Volume III, ed. Harry Alonso Cushing (Amazon Kindle), Kindle Location 7 percent of 100.

[32] Samuel Adams "The Committee of Correspondence of Boston to Inhabitants of the Province of Quebec, 1775" in The Writings of Samuel Adams Volume III, ed. Harry Alonso Cushing (Amazon Kindle), Kindle Location 46 percent of 100.

[33] Samuel Adams "Letter to George Read, 1775" in The Writings of Samuel Adams Volume III, ed. Harry Alonso Cushing (Amazon Kindle), Kindle Location 48 percent of 100.

[34] Samuel Adams "Candidus, 1776" in The Writings of Samuel Adams Volume III, ed. Harry Alonso Cushing (Amazon Kindle), Kindle Location 65 percent of 100.

"Ne'er yet by force was freedom overcome." [35] - Samuel Adams

"We trust in God, & in the Smiles of Heaven on the Justice of our Cause, that a Day is hastening, when the Efforts of the Colonists will be crowned with Success; and the present Generation furnish an Example of publick Virtue, worthy the Imitation of all Posterity."[36] - Samuel Adams

"Where did you learn that in a state or society you had a right to do as you please? And that it was an infringement of that right to restrain you? This is a refinement which I dare say, the true sons of liberty despise."[37] - Samuel Adams

"It is in the Interest of Tyrants to reduce the People to Ignorance and Vice. For they cannot live in any Country where Virtue and Knowledge prevail. The Religion and public Liberty of a People are intimately connected; their Interests are interwoven, they cannot subsist separately; and therefore they rise and fall together. For this Reason, it is always observable, that those who are combin'd to destroy the People's liberties, practice every Art to poison their Morals."[38] - Samuel Adams

"Religion has been & I hope will continue to be the ornament of N. England. While they place their Confidence in God they will not fail to be an happy People."[39] - Samuel Adams

"The diminution of publick Virtue is usually attended with that of publick Happiness, and the publick Liberty will not long survive the total Extinction of Morals."[40] - Samuel Adams

"I have long been convinced that our Enemies have made it an Object, to eradicate from the Minds of the People in general a Sense of true Religion & Virtue, in hopes thereby the more easily to carry their Point of enslaving them."[41] - Samuel Adams

"After all, virtue is the surest means of securing the public liberty."[42] - Samuel Adams

"We owe our grateful Acknowledgments to him who is, as he is frequently stiled in sacred Writ "The Lord of Hosts" "The God of Armies"..."[43] - Samuel Adams

---

[35] Samuel Adams "Candidus, 1771" in The Writings of Samuel Adams Volume II, ed. Harry Alonso Cushing (Amazon Kindle), Kindle Location 56 percent of 100.
[36] Samuel Adams "The Committee of Correspondence of Boston to the Committee of Cambridge, 1772" in The Writings of Samuel Adams Volume II, ed. Harry Alonso Cushing (Amazon Kindle), Kindle Location 86 percent of 100.
[37] Samuel Adams "Determinatus, 1770" in The Writings of Samuel Adams Volume II, ed. Harry Alonso Cushing (Amazon Kindle), Kindle Location 2 percent of 100.
[38] Samuel Adams "Valerius Poplicola, 1772" in The Writings of Samuel Adams Volume II, ed. Harry Alonso Cushing (Amazon Kindle), Kindle Location 73 percent of 100.
[39] Samuel Adams "Letter to Mrs. Samuel [Betsy] Adams, 1777" in The Writings of Samuel Adams Volume III, ed. Harry Alonso Cushing (Amazon Kindle), Kindle Location 98 percent of 100.
[40] Samuel Adams "Letter to John Scollay, 1776" in The Writings of Samuel Adams Volume III, ed. Harry Alonso Cushing (Amazon Kindle), Kindle Location 69 percent of 100.
[41] Ibid.
[42] Samuel Adams "Letter to Elbridge Gerry, 1775" in The Writings of Samuel Adams Volume III, ed. Harry Alonso Cushing (Amazon Kindle), Kindle Location 57 percent of 100.
[43] Samuel Adams "Letter to Joseph Palmer, 1776" in The Writings of Samuel Adams Volume III, ed. Harry Alonso Cushing (Amazon Kindle), Kindle Location 66 percent of 100.

"But an immoral man, for instance one who will commonly prophane the name of his maker, certainly cannot be esteemed of equal credit by a jury, with one who fears to take that sacred name in vain: It is impossible he should in the mind of any man..."[44] - Samuel Adams

"All positive and civil laws, should conform as far as possible, to the Law of natural reason and equity."[45] - Samuel Adams

"It is agreed to appoint a Day of Prayer, & a Come [someone] will bring in a Resolution for that purpose this day."[46] - Samuel Adams

"If the liberties of America are ever compleatly ruined...it will in all probability be the consequence of a mistaken notion of prudence, which leads men to acquiesce in measures of the most destructive tendency for the sake of the present ease."[47] - Samuel Adams

"If the youth are carefully educated - If the Principles of Morality are strongly inculcated on the Minds of the People - the End and Design of Government clearly understood and the Love of our Country the ruling Passion, uncorrupted Men will then be chosen for the representatives of the People."[48] - Samuel Adams

"Revelation assures us that "Righteousness exalteth a Nation" - Communities are dealt with in this World by the wise and just Ruler of the Universe. He rewards or punishes them according to their general Character."[49] - Samuel Adams

"It is my most fervent prayer to Almighty God, that he would direct and prosper the Councils of America, inspire her Armies with true Courage, shield them in every Instant of Danger and lead them on to Victory & Tryumph."[50] - Samuel Adams

"The Man who is conscientiously doing his Duty will ever be protected by that Righteous and all powerful Being, and when he has finished his Work he will receive an ample Reward."[51] - Samuel Adams

---

[44] Samuel Adams "Vindex, 1771" in The Writings of Samuel Adams Volume II, ed. Harry Alonso Cushing (Amazon Kindle), Kindle Location 32 percent of 100.

[45] Samuel Adams "The Rights of The Colonists, a List of Violations of Rights and a Letter of Correspondence, 1772" in The Writings of Samuel Adams Volume II, ed. Harry Alonso Cushing (Amazon Kindle), Kindle Location 76 percent of 100.

[46] Samuel Adams "Letter to Mrs. Samuel [Betsy] Adams, 1776" in The Writings of Samuel Adams Volume III, ed. Harry Alonso Cushing (Amazon Kindle), Kindle Location 79 percent of 100.

[47] Samuel Adams "Candidus, 1771" in The Writings of Samuel Adams Volume II, ed. Harry Alonso Cushing (Amazon Kindle), Kindle Location 63 percent of 100.

[48] Samuel Adams "Letter to James Warren, 1775" in The Writings of Samuel Adams Volume III, ed. Harry Alonso Cushing (Amazon Kindle), Kindle Location 60 percent of 100.

[49] Samuel Adams "Letter to John Scollay, 1776" in The Writings of Samuel Adams Volume III, ed. Harry Alonso Cushing (Amazon Kindle), Kindle Location 69 percent of 100.

[50] Samuel Adams "Letter to James Sullivan, 1776" in The Writings of Samuel Adams Volume III, ed. Harry Alonso Cushing (Amazon Kindle), Kindle Location 62 percent of 100.

[51] Samuel Adams "Letter to Mrs. Samuel [Betsy] Adams, 1776" in The Writings of Samuel Adams Volume III, ed. Harry Alonso Cushing (Amazon Kindle), Kindle Location 84 percent of 100.

"I hope my Countrymen have been wise in their Elections and I pray God to bless their Endeavors for the establishment of publick Liberty Virtue & Happiness."[52] - Samuel Adams

"He who should not have employed bad Men, or at least should have restrained or punished them, incurred the same Censure as if he himself had done it!"[53] - Samuel Adams

"It can never be expected that a people, however NUMEROUS, will form & execute a wise plan to perpetuate their Liberty, when they have lost the Spirit & feeling of it."[54] - Samuel Adams

"I confess, I have a strong desire that our Colony should excell in Wisdom and Virtue."[55] - Samuel Adams

"Could I be assured that America would remain virtuous, I would venture to defy the utmost Efforts of Enemies to subjugate her."[56] - Samuel Adams

"One would from this & other like Instances conclude, that to be possessed of the Christian Principles, & to accommodate our whole Deportment to such Principles, is to be happy in this Life, it is this that sweetens every thing we enjoy; indeed of it self it yields us full Satisfaction, & thus puts it out of the power of the World to disappoint us by any of its frowns."[57] – Samuel Adams

"May God give us Wisdom Fortitude Perseverance and every other virtue necessary for us to maintain that Independence which we have asserted."[58] - Samuel Adams

"My daily Prayer is for your Safety, & Happiness in this Life & a better. Adieu, my dear."[59] - Samuel Adams

"...but the Language of the people is, "In the Name of the Lord we will tread down our Enemies.""[60] - Samuel Adams

On Judicial Limits and Law:

---

[52] Samuel Adams "Letter to James Warren, 1777" in The Writings of Samuel Adams Volume III, ed. Harry Alonso Cushing (Amazon Kindle), Kindle Location 89 percent of 100.

[53] Samuel Adams "A Chatterer, 1770" in The Writings of Samuel Adams Volume II, ed. Harry Alonso Cushing (Amazon Kindle), Kindle Location 9 percent of 100.

[54] Samuel Adams "A The Committee of Correspondence of Boston to Other Committees, 1773" in The Writings of Samuel Adams Volume III, ed. Harry Alonso Cushing (Amazon Kindle), Kindle Location 19 percent of 100.

[55] Samuel Adams "Letter to James Warren, 1775" in The Writings of Samuel Adams Volume III, ed. Harry Alonso Cushing (Amazon Kindle), Kindle Location 60 percent of 100

[56] Samuel Adams "Letter to John Scollay, 1776" in The Writings of Samuel Adams Volume III, ed. Harry Alonso Cushing (Amazon Kindle), Kindle Location 69 percent of 100.

[57] Samuel Adams "Letter to Andrew Elton Wells, 1772" in The Writings of Samuel Adams Volume II, ed. Harry Alonso Cushing (Amazon Kindle), Kindle Location 74 percent of 100.

[58] Samuel Adams "Letter to John Adams, 1776" in The Writings of Samuel Adams Volume III, ed. Harry Alonso Cushing (Amazon Kindle), Kindle Location 75 percent of 100.

[59] Samuel Adams "Letter to Mrs. Samuel [Betsy] Adams, 1776" in The Writings of Samuel Adams Volume III, ed. Harry Alonso Cushing (Amazon Kindle), Kindle Location 78 percent of 100.

[60] Samuel Adams "Letter to Arthur Lee, 1775" in The Writings of Samuel Adams Volume III, ed. Harry Alonso Cushing (Amazon Kindle), Kindle Location 50 percent of 100.

"It was formerly the saying of an English Tyrant "Let me have Judges at my Command & make what Laws you please."[61] - Samuel Adams

"All positive and civil laws, should conform as far as possible, to the Law of natural reason and equity."[62] - Samuel Adams

"They [the legislature] ought to consider the fundamental [constitutional] laws as sacred, if the nation has not in very express terms, given them the power to change them."[63] - Samuel Adams

"It is a pitiful constitution indeed, which so far from being fixed and permanent as it should be - sacred and unalterable in the hands of those where the community has placed it, depends entirely upon the breath of a minister [of state], or of any man..."[64] - Samuel Adams

"...But when state-lawyers, attorneys and sollicitors general, & persons advanced to the highest stations in the courts of the law, prostitute the honor of the profession, become the tools of ministers [of state], and employ their talents for explaining away, if possible the Rights of a kingdom, they are then the proper objects of the odium and indignation of the public."[65] - Samuel Adams

"If men through fear, fraud or mistake, should in terms renounce and give up any essential natural right, the eternal law of reason and the great end of society, would absolutely vacate such renunciation; the right to freedom being the gift of God Almighty, it is not in the power of Man to alienate this gift, and voluntarily become a slave..."[66] - Samuel Adams

On Economic and Tax Policy:

"The restraining us from erecting Stilling Mills for manufacturing our Iron the natural produce of this Country, Is an infringement of that right with which God and nature have invested us, to make use of our skill and industry in procuring the necessaries and conveniences of life."[67] - Samuel Adams

"Whatever laws therefore are made in a society, tending to render property insecure, must be subversive of the end for which men prefer society to the state of nature..."[68] - Samuel Adams

---

[61] Samuel Adams "Committee of Correspondence of Boston to Elijah Morton, 1773" in The Writings of Samuel Adams Volume III, ed. Harry Alonso Cushing (Amazon Kindle), Kindle Location 13 percent of 100.

[62] Samuel Adams "The Rights of The Colonists, a List of Violations of Rights and a Letter of Correspondence, 1772" in The Writings of Samuel Adams Volume II, ed. Harry Alonso Cushing (Amazon Kindle), Kindle Location 76 percent of 100.

[63] Samuel Adams "Letter to the Governor, 1773" in The Writings of Samuel Adams Volume II, ed. Harry Alonso Cushing (Amazon Kindle), Kindle Location 92 percent of 100.

[64] Samuel Adams "Candidus, 1771" in The Writings of Samuel Adams Volume II, ed. Harry Alonso Cushing (Amazon Kindle), Kindle Location 50 percent of 100.

[65] Samuel Adams "A Chatterer, 1770" in The Writings of Samuel Adams Volume II, ed. Harry Alonso Cushing (Amazon Kindle), Kindle Location 10 percent of 100.

[66] Samuel Adams "The Rights of The Colonists, a List of Violations of Rights and a Letter of Correspondence, 1772" in The Writings of Samuel Adams Volume II, ed. Harry Alonso Cushing (Amazon Kindle), Kindle Location 77 percent of 100.

[67] Samuel Adams "The Rights of The Colonists, a List of Violations of Rights and a Letter of Correspondence, 1772" in The Writings of Samuel Adams Volume II, ed. Harry Alonso Cushing (Amazon Kindle), Kindle Location 80 percent of 100.

On Personal and National Defense:

"Or is he at length become wise enough to attend to a good old Maxim, IN PEACE PREPARE FOR WAR."[69] - Samuel Adams

"...Certainly no persons could be tho't blame-worthy, for pursuing a banditti, who had already put a number of peaceable people in great terror of their lives, with a design to prevent their doing further mischief..."[70] - Samuel Adams

"After the Example of those renowned Heroes, whose memory we revere, let us gloriously defend our Rights & Liberites (sic), & resolve to transmit the fair Inheritance they purchased for us with Treasure & Blood to their latest posterity."[71] - Samuel Adams

"The People are recollecting the Achievements of their Ancestors and whenever it shall be necessary for them to draw their Swords in the Defence of their Liberties, they will shew themselves to be worthy of such Ancestors."[72] - Samuel Adams

"The publick Liberty must be preserved though at the Expense of Lives!"[73] - Samuel Adams

"Could I be assured that America would remain virtuous, I would venture to defy the utmost Efforts of Enemies to subjugate her."[74] - Samuel Adams

On American Exceptionalism and the Future of America:

"It requires but a small portion of the gift of discernment for any one to foresee, that providence will erect a mighty empire in America..."[75] - Samuel Adams

---

[68] Samuel Adams "Candidus, 1772" in The Writings of Samuel Adams Volume II, ed. Harry Alonso Cushing (Amazon Kindle), Kindle Location 69 percent of 100.

[69] Samuel Adams "Letter to Samuel Cooper, 1777" in The Writings of Samuel Adams Volume III, ed. Harry Alonso Cushing (Amazon Kindle), Kindle Location 85 percent of 100.

[70] Samuel Adams "Vindex, 1771" in The Writings of Samuel Adams Volume II, ed. Harry Alonso Cushing (Amazon Kindle), Kindle Location 29 percent of 100.

[71] Samuel Adams "Committee of Correspondence of Boston to John Wadsworth, 1773" in The Writings of Samuel Adams Volume III, ed. Harry Alonso Cushing (Amazon Kindle), Kindle Location 11 percent of 100.

[72] Samuel Adams "Letter to Arthur Lee, 1775" in The Writings of Samuel Adams Volume III, ed. Harry Alonso Cushing (Amazon Kindle), Kindle Location 44 percent of 100.

[73] Samuel Adams "Letter to Arthur Lee, 1775" in The Writings of Samuel Adams Volume III, ed. Harry Alonso Cushing (Amazon Kindle), Kindle Location 49 percent of 100.

[74] Samuel Adams "Letter to John Scollay, 1776" in The Writings of Samuel Adams Volume III, ed. Harry Alonso Cushing (Amazon Kindle), Kindle Location 69 percent of 100.

[75] Samuel Adams "Letter to Arthur Lee, 1774" in The Writings of Samuel Adams Volume III, ed. Harry Alonso Cushing (Amazon Kindle), Kindle Location 28 percent of 100.

George Washington, Quotes for Conservatives and Republicans

The lives of many of history's great figures are best viewed at a distance. Their stories become less extraordinary when the details are examined.

What is fascinating about Washington is that his character becomes more amazing the more closely one looks. That is not to say that he did not have flaws or make mistakes – there were plenty of both. But when the moment came to make truly crucial decisions, both his leadership – and his personal integrity – remained strong.

His election as the first president of the United States was the only unanimous choice for that post in American history (Ronald Reagan came close, winning the vote in forty-nine states out of fifty).

Washington gained the trust of the people more for his willingness to give up power than for his desire to wield it. Alexander Hamilton, another Founding Father and Washington's chief of staff, wanted Washington to become the King of the United States. Washington had no interest in such a post. At one point during the war, many hoped that Washington would use the Continental Army to force the hand of Congress (Congress had failed to provide the Army with adequate supplies). He refused.

Many years later, at the end of his second term as president, Washington was begged to run for a third term. Although his electoral victory would have been certain, he went back to his home at Mount Vernon. Like a true father, he knew that his young country needed to learn to stand on its own.

That level of modesty would have been surprising in a lesser man, but Washington's accomplishments gave him as much a right to arrogance and conceit as anyone. With a ragtag band of poorly equipped and poorly trained soldiers, whose instruction in basic military discipline (by the Baron von Steuben) came only once the war was well underway, and with no navy to speak of, Washington beat the British - the finest military force on earth – thus securing American Independence.

After the war, Washington served in a post no less prestigious than the president of the Constitutional Convention. The convention produced a document that, two-hundred and thirty years later, is still the legal foundation of our republic. During his subsequent presidency, Washington was eminently successful, managing to unite a fractious nation with deft diplomacy and straightforward American style. He also kept it safe – all while setting daily precedents for an office that had never existed before.

The quotes below show the close similarity between Washington's ideas and those of modern Republicans and conservatives.

On National Debt:

"As a very important source of strength and security, cherish public credit."[76] - George Washington

"Allow me, moreover, to hope that it will be a favorite policy with you, not merely to secure a payment of the interest of the debt funded, but as far and as fast as the growing resources of the country will permit to exonerate it of the principal itself."[77] - George Washington

"Whatsoever will tend to accelerate the honorable extinction of our public debt accords as much with the true interest of our country as with the general sense of our constituents."[78] - George Washington

"No pecuniary consideration is more urgent than the regular redemption and discharge of the public debt."[79] - George Washington

On National Defense:

"To be prepared for war is one of the most effectual means of preserving peace."[80] - George Washington

"There is a rank due to the United States among nations which will be withheld, if not absolutely lost, by the reputation of weakness."[81] - George Washington

"If we desire to avoid insult, we must be able to repel it; if we desire to secure peace, one of the most powerful instruments of our rising prosperity, it must be known that we are at all times ready for war."[82] - George Washington

"Among the many interesting objects which will engage your attention that of providing for the common defense will merit particular regard."[83] - George Washington

"The safety of the United States under divine protection ought to rest on the basis of systematic and solid arrangements, exposed as little as possible to the hazards of fortuitous circumstances."[84] - George Washington

"To secure respect to a neutral flag requires a naval force organized and ready to vindicate it from insult or aggression."[85] - George Washington

---

[76] George Washington "Farewell Address, 1796" in The American Republic Primary Sources, ed. Bruce Frohnen (Indianapolis: Liberty Fund, Inc., 2002), p. 77.

[77] George Washington "State of the Union Address, Jan. 8, 1790" in State of the Union Address, George Washington, A Public Domain Book, (Amazon Kindle), Kindle Location 14 percent of 100.

[78] George Washington "State of the Union Address, Dec. 8, 1795" in State of the Union Address, George Washington, A Public Domain Book, (Amazon Kindle), Kindle Location 81 percent of 100.

[79] George Washington "State of the Union Address, Dec. 3, 1793" in State of the Union Address, George Washington, A Public Domain Book, (Amazon Kindle), Kindle Location 51 percent of 100.

[80] George Washington "State of the Union Address, Jan. 8, 1790" in State of the Union Address, George Washington, A Public Domain Book, (Amazon Kindle), Kindle Location 1 percent of 100.

[81] George Washington "State of the Union Address, Dec. 3, 1793" in State of the Union Address, George Washington, A Public Domain Book, (Amazon Kindle), Kindle Location 46 percent of 100.

[82] Ibid.

[83] George Washington "State of the Union Address, Jan. 8, 1790" in State of the Union Address, George Washington, A Public Domain Book, (Amazon Kindle), Kindle Location 1 percent of 100.

[84] George Washington "State of the Union Address, Oct. 25, 1791" in State of the Union Address, George Washington, A Public Domain Book, (Amazon Kindle), Kindle Location 27 percent of 100.

"To an active external commerce the protection of a naval force is indispensable." - George Washington

On Immigration:

"Various considerations also render it expedient that the terms on which foreigners may be admitted to the rights of citizens should be speedily ascertained by a uniform rule of naturalization."[86] - George Washington

On the Constitution:

"But the Constitution which at any time exists, 'till changed by an explicit and authentic act of the whole people, is sacredly obligatory upon all."[87] - George Washington

"...let them persevere in their affectionate vigilance over that precious depository of American happiness, the Constitution of the United States."[88] - George Washington

"It is important, likewise, that the habits of thinking in a free Country should inspire caution in those entrusted with its administration, to confine themselves within their respective Constitutional spheres; avoiding in the exercise of the Powers of one department to encroach upon another."[89] - George Washington

On Religion and Government:

"Can it be, that Providence has not connected the permanent felicity of a Nation with its virtue?"[90] - George Washington

"Of all the dispositions and habits which lead to political prosperity, Religion and morality are indispensable supports. In vain would that man claim the tribute of Patriotism, who should labour to subvert these great pillars of human happiness, these firmest props of the duties of Men and citizens."[91] - George Washington

---

[85] George Washington "State of the Union Address, Dec. 7, 1796" in State of the Union Address, George Washington, A Public Domain Book, (Amazon Kindle), Kindle Location 88 percent of 100.
[86] George Washington "State of the Union Address, Jan. 8, 1790" in State of the Union Address, George Washington, A Public Domain Book, (Amazon Kindle), Kindle Location 3 percent of 100.
[87] George Washington "Farewell Address, 1796" in The American Republic Primary Sources, ed. Bruce Frohnen (Indianapolis: Liberty Fund, Inc., 2002), p. 74.
[88] George Washington "State of the Union Address, Nov. 19, 1794" in State of the Union Address, George Washington, A Public Domain Book, (Amazon Kindle), Kindle Location 65 percent of 100.
[89] George Washington "Farewell Address, 1796" in The American Republic Primary Sources, ed. Bruce Frohnen (Indianapolis: Liberty Fund, Inc., 2002), p. 76.
[90] George Washington "Farewell Address, 1796" in The American Republic Primary Sources, ed. Bruce Frohnen (Indianapolis: Liberty Fund, Inc., 2002), p. 77.
[91] George Washington "Farewell Address, 1796" in The American Republic Primary Sources, ed. Bruce Frohnen (Indianapolis: Liberty Fund, Inc., 2002), p. 76.

"Whatever may be conceded to the influence of refined education on minds of peculiar structure, reason and experience both forbid us to expect that National morality can prevail in exclusion of religious principle."[92] - George Washington

"America, under the smiles of a Divine Providence, the protection of a good government, and the cultivation of manners, morals, and piety, cannot fail of attaining an un-common degree of eminence..."[93] - George Washington

"Now therefore I do recommend and assign Thursday the 26th. day of November next to be devoted by the People of these States to the service of that great and glorious Being, who is the beneficent Author of all the good that was, that is, or that will be."[94] - George Washington

"Fellow-Citizens of the Senate and House of Representatives: In recurring to the internal situation of our country since I had last the pleasure to address you, I find ample reason for a renewed expression of that gratitude to the Ruler of the Universe which a continued series of prosperity has so often and so justly called forth."[95] - George Washington

On Personal Industry:

"Numerous as are the providential blessings which demand our grateful acknowledgments, the abundance with which another year has again rewarded the industry of the husbandman is too important to escape recollection."[96] - George Washington

On American Exceptionalism:

"...is it too much to say that our country exhibits a spectacle of national happiness never surpassed, if ever before equaled?"[97] - George Washington

---

[92] George Washington "Farewell Address, 1796" in The American Republic Primary Sources, ed. Bruce Frohnen (Indianapolis: Liberty Fund, Inc., 2002), p. 76.

[93] George Washington "Letter to the Roman Catholics in the United States of America, 1790" in The American Republic Primary Sources, ed. Bruce Frohnen (Indianapolis: Liberty Fund, Inc., 2002), p. 70.

[94] George Washington "Thanksgiving Proclamation, 1789" in The American Republic Primary Sources, ed. Bruce Frohnen (Indianapolis: Liberty Fund, Inc., 2002), p. 69.

[95] George Washington "State of the Union Address, Dec. 7, 1796" in State of the Union Address, George Washington, A Public Domain Book, (Amazon Kindle), Kindle Location 83 percent of 100.

[96] George Washington "State of the Union Address, Oct. 25, 1791" in State of the Union Address, George Washington, A Public Domain Book, (Amazon Kindle), Kindle Location 16 percent of 100.

[97] George Washington "State of the Union Address, Dec. 8, 1795" in State of the Union Address, George Washington, A Public Domain Book, (Amazon Kindle), Kindle Location 76 percent of 100.

John and Abigail Adams Quotes for Conservatives and Republicans

It is easy to argue about the importance which we should assign to each of our founding fathers, but difficult to place John Adams very far down the list. His words are well worth reading as a part of any attempt to determine which values have allowed America to prosper in both freedom and opportunity.

Adams was involved in practically every major aspect of America's independence movement and early statehood.

After the Boston Massacre, an event that meant a great deal to advocates of independence, he successfully defended in court the British troops who had fired on American colonists. Though unpopular at the time, this helped make the face of the impending revolution one of principle, rather than politics.

Elected as a delegate to the Continental Congress that had been established to deal with the difficulties the Colonies were having with the British, Adams "emerged as one of the most "sensible and forcible" figures in the whole patriot cause...his influence exceeding even that of his better-known kinsman...Samuel Adams."[98]

Although Thomas Jefferson is often cited as having written the Declaration of Independence, in reality the task was assigned to a committee of five men, including Adams. Though Jefferson was the primary author, he likely consulted with Adams more than with anyone else on the document's drafts. [99] Adams was also the "chief advocate" for the passage of the declaration "on the floor of Congress."[100]

During the revolution, Adams was one of America's diplomats to France, and later one of three American signers of the Treaty of Paris, in which the British recognized what was already an accomplished fact – American independence. After the revolution was over, Adams became George Washington's vice president, and, later, America's second president.

The following quotes illustrate his ideas, and those of his brilliant wife, Abigail - from whose correspondence with her husband many of his quotes derive

Religion, Morals, Civil Society and Their Effect on Government:

"It would be unbecoming the representatives of this nation to assemble for the first time in this solemn temple without looking up to the Supreme Ruler of the Universe and imploring His blessing."[101] - John Adams

---

[98] McCullough, John Adams. p. 20.

[99] McCullough, John Adams. P. 643.

[100] Ibid.

[101] John Adams "State of the Union Address, Nov. 11, 1800" in State of the Union Address, John Adams, A Public Domain Book, (Amazon Kindle), Kindle Location 82 percent of 100.

"Here and throughout our country may simple manners, pure morals, and true religion flourish forever."[102] John Adams

"Liberty can no more exist without virtue and independence, than the body can live and move without a soul."[103] - John Adams

"Congress have appointed two chaplains, Mr. White and Mr. Duffield, the former of whom, an Episcopalian, is arrived, and opens Congress with prayers every day. The latter is expected every hour."[104] John Adams

"...we have abundant reason to present to the Supreme Being our annual oblations of gratitude for a liberal participation in the ordinary blessings of His providence."[105] - John Adams

"The freedom of thinking was never yet extended in any country so far as the utter subversion of all religion and morality, nor as the abolition of the laws and constitution of the country."[106] - John Adams

"If there is a form of government, then, whose principle and foundation is virtue, will not every sober man acknowledge it better calculated to promote the general happiness than any other form?" [107] - John Adams

"We have appointed a Continental fast. Millions will be upon their knees at once before their great Creator, imploring his forgiveness and blessing; his smiles on American councils and arms."[108] John Adams

"It [Independence Day] ought to be commemorated as the day of deliverance, by solemn acts of devotion to God Almighty."[109] - John Adams

"Dr. [Franklin] proposes a device for a seal: Moses lifting up his wand and dividing the Red Sea, and the Pharaoh in his chariot overwhelmed with the waters. This motto, "Rebellion to tyrants is obedience to God."[110] - John Adams

---

[102] John Adams "State of the Union Address, Nov. 11, 1800" in State of the Union Address, John Adams, A Public Domain Book, (Amazon Kindle), Kindle Location 83 percent of 100.

[103] John Adams "Novanglus Essays" in John Adams, Works, (The Perfect Library), (Amazon Kindle), Kindle Location 17 percent of 100.

[104] John Adams "Letter to Abigail" in Familiar Letters of John Adams and His Wife Abigail Adams During the Revolution, ed. Charles Francis Adams (New York: Hurd and Houghton, 1875). A Public Domain Book, (Amazon Kindle), Kindle Location 78 percent of 100.

[105] John Adams "State of the Union Address, Dec. 8, 1798" in State of the Union Address, John Adams, A Public Domain Book, (Amazon Kindle), Kindle Location 32 percent of 100.

[106] John Adams "Novanglus Essays" in John Adams, Works, (The Perfect Library), (Amazon Kindle), Kindle Location 44 percent of 100.

[107] John Adams "Thoughts on Government" in John Adams, Works, (The Perfect Library), (Amazon Kindle), Kindle Location 81 percent of 100.

[108] John Adams "Letter to Abigail" in Familiar Letters of John Adams and His Wife Abigail Adams During the Revolution, ed. Charles Francis Adams (New York: Hurd and Houghton, 1875). A Public Domain Book, (Amazon Kindle), Kindle Location 20 percent of 100.

[109] John Adams "Letter to Abigail" in Familiar Letters of John Adams and His Wife Abigail Adams During the Revolution, ed. Charles Francis Adams (New York: Hurd and Houghton, 1875). A Public Domain Book, (Amazon Kindle), Kindle Location 49 percent of 100.

"The clergy of this province are a virtuous, sensible, and learned set of men, and they do not take their sermons from newspapers, but the Bible; unless it be a few, who preach passive obedience."[111] - John Adams

"Certainly there is a Providence; certainly we must depend upon Providence, or we fail; certainly the sincere prayers of good men avail much."[112] John Adams

"...we have, nevertheless, abundant cause of gratitude to the source of benevolence..."[113] - John Adams

"...the welfare and prosperity of all countries, communities, and, I may add, individuals, depend upon their morals."[114] Abigail Adams

"For, however the belief of a particular Providence may be exploded by the modern wits, and the infidelity of too many of the rising generation deride the idea, yet the virtuous mind will look up and acknowledge the great First Cause, without whose notice not even a sparrow falls to the ground." "I know America capable of anything she undertakes with spirit and vigor."[115] - Abigail Adams

American Enterprise and Economics:

"In short, commerce has made this country what it is, and it can not be destroyed or neglected without involving the people in poverty and distress."[116] - John Adams

"The commerce of the United States is essential, if not to their existence, at least to their comfort, their growth, prosperity, and happiness. The genius, character, and habits of the people are highly commercial."[117] - John Adams

On Public Debt:

---

[110] John Adams "Letter to Abigail" in Familiar Letters of John Adams and His Wife Abigail Adams During the Revolution, ed. Charles Francis Adams (New York: Hurd and Houghton, 1875). A Public Domain Book, (Amazon Kindle), Kindle Location 53 percent of 100.

[111] John Adams "Novanglus Essays" in John Adams, Works, (The Perfect Library), (Amazon Kindle), Kindle Location 16 percent of 100.

[112]John Adams "Letter to Abigail" in Familiar Letters of John Adams and His Wife Abigail Adams During the Revolution, ed. Charles Francis Adams (New York: Hurd and Houghton, 1875). A Public Domain Book, (Amazon Kindle), Kindle Location 12 percent of 100.

[113] John Adams "State of the Union Address, Nov. 22, 1797" in State of the Union Address, John Adams, A Public Domain Book, (Amazon Kindle), Kindle Location 3 percent of 100.

[114] Abigail Adams "Letter to John" in Familiar Letters of John Adams and His Wife Abigail Adams During the Revolution, ed. Charles Francis Adams (New York: Hurd and Houghton, 1875). A Public Domain Book, (Amazon Kindle), Kindle Location 82 percent of 100.

[115] Abigail Adams "Letter to John" in Familiar Letters of John Adams and His Wife Abigail Adams During the Revolution, ed. Charles Francis Adams (New York: Hurd and Houghton, 1875). A Public Domain Book, (Amazon Kindle), Kindle Location 93 percent of 100.

[116] John Adams "State of the Union Address, Nov. 22, 1797" in State of the Union Address, John Adams, A Public Domain Book, (Amazon Kindle), Kindle Location 9 percent of 100.

[117] John Adams "State of the Union Address, Nov. 22, 1797" in State of the Union Address, John Adams, A Public Domain Book, (Amazon Kindle), Kindle Location 8 percent of 100.

"The consequences arising from the continual accumulation of public debts in other countries ought to admonish us to be careful to prevent their growth in our own."[118] - John Adams

"The revenue creates pensioners, and the pensioners urge for more revenue."[119] - John Adams

"The preservation of public credit, the regular extinguishment of the public debt, and a provision of funds to defray any extraordinary expenses will of course call for your serious attention."[120] - John Adams

On National Defense:

"An efficient preparation for war can alone insure peace."[121] - John Adams

"A manly sense of national honor, dignity, and independence has appeared which, if encouraged and invigorated by every branch of the government, will enable us to view undismayed the enterprises of any foreign power and become the sure foundation of national prosperity and glory."[122] - John Adams

"...nothing short of the power of repelling aggressions will secure to our country a rational prospect of escaping the calamities of war or national degradation."[123] - John Adams

"Yet we are told that all the misfortunes of Sparta were occasioned by their too great solicitude for present tranquillity, and, from an excessive love of peace, they neglected the means of making it sure and lasting."[124] - John Adams

"We can not, without committing a dangerous imprudence, abandon those measures of self protection which are adapted to our situation and to which, notwithstanding our pacific policy, the violence and injustice of others may again compel us to resort."[125] - John Adams

Limited Government:

---

[118] John Adams "State of the Union Address, Nov. 22, 1797" in State of the Union Address, John Adams, A Public Domain Book, (Amazon Kindle), Kindle Location 25, 26percent of 100.

[119] John Adams "Novanglus Essays" in John Adams, Works, (The Perfect Library), (Amazon Kindle), Kindle Location 16 percent of 100.

[120] John Adams "XYZ Message to Congress" in John Adams, Works, (The Perfect Library), (Amazon Kindle), Kindle Location 93 percent of 100.

[121] John Adams "State of the Union Address, Dec. 8, 1798" in State of the Union Address, John Adams, A Public Domain Book, (Amazon Kindle), Kindle Location 40 percent of 100.

[122] John Adams "State of the Union Address, Dec. 8, 1798" in State of the Union Address, John Adams, A Public Domain Book, (Amazon Kindle), Kindle Location 33 percent of 100.

[123] John Adams "State of the Union Address, Dec. 3, 1799" in State of the Union Address, John Adams, A Public Domain Book, (Amazon Kindle), Kindle Location 79 percent of 100.

[124] John Adams "Letter to Abigail" in Familiar Letters of John Adams and His Wife Abigail Adams During the Revolution, ed. Charles Francis Adams (New York: Hurd and Houghton, 1875). A Public Domain Book, (Amazon Kindle), Kindle Location 12 percent of 100.

[125] John Adams "State of the Union Address, Nov. 11, 1800" in State of the Union Address, John Adams, A Public Domain Book, (Amazon Kindle), Kindle Location 91 percent of 100.

"Obsta principiis, nip the shoots of arbitrary power in the bud, is the only maxim which can ever preserve the liberties of any people."[126] - John Adams

"Liberty, once lost, is lost forever."[127] John Adams

"When the people once surrender their share in the legislature, and their right of defending the limitations upon the Government, and of resisting every encroachment upon them, they can never regain it."[128] John Adams

"A settled plan to deprive the people of all the benefits, blessings, and ends of the contract, to subvert the fundamentals of the constitution, to deprive them of all share in making and executing laws, will justify a revolution."[129] - John Adams

"...if a continental constitution should be formed, it should be a congress...and its authority should sacredly be confined to these cases, namely, war, trade, disputes between colony and colony, the post office, and the unappropriated lands of the crown, as they used to be called."[130] - John Adams

"...the service of the public ought to be an honorary, rather than a lucrative employment..."[131] - John Adams

"A single assembly is apt to be avaricious, and in time will not scruple to exempt itself from burdens, which it will lay, without compunction, on its constituents."[132] - John Adams

"It has been a warning to their posterity, and one principal motive with the people never to trust any agent with power to concede away their privileges again."[133] - John Adams

"'T is [sic] a maxim of state, that power and liberty are like heat and moisture. Where they are well mixed, everything prospers; where they are single, they are destructive."[134] - Abigail Adams

---

[126] John Adams "Novanglus Essays" in John Adams, Works, (The Perfect Library), (Amazon Kindle), Kindle Location 22 percent of 100.

[127] John Adams "Letter to Abigail" in Familiar Letters of John Adams and His Wife Abigail Adams During the Revolution, ed. Charles Francis Adams (New York: Hurd and Houghton, 1875). A Public Domain Book, (Amazon Kindle), Kindle Location 23 percent of 100.

[128] John Adams "Letter to Abigail" in Familiar Letters of John Adams and His Wife Abigail Adams During the Revolution, ed. Charles Francis Adams (New York: Hurd and Houghton, 1875). A Public Domain Book, (Amazon Kindle), Kindle Location 23 percent of 100.

[129] John Adams "Novanglus Essays" in John Adams, Works, (The Perfect Library), (Amazon Kindle), Kindle Location 10 percent of 100.

[130] John Adams "Thoughts on Government" in John Adams, Works, (The Perfect Library), (Amazon Kindle), Kindle Location 84 percent of 100.

[131]John Adams "Novanglus Essays" in John Adams, Works, (The Perfect Library), (Amazon Kindle), Kindle Location 34 percent of 100.

[132] John Adams "Thoughts on Government" in John Adams, Works, (The Perfect Library), (Amazon Kindle), Kindle Location 82 percent of 100.

[133] John Adams "Novanglus Essays" in John Adams, Works, (The Perfect Library), (Amazon Kindle), Kindle Location 57 percent of 100.

[134] Abigail Adams "Letter to John" in Familiar Letters of John Adams and His Wife Abigail Adams During the Revolution, ed. Charles Francis Adams (New York: Hurd and Houghton, 1875). A Public Domain Book, (Amazon Kindle), Kindle Location 44 percent of 100.

"We ought to be cautious of the inaccuracies of the greatest men, for these are apt to lead us astray."[135] - John Adams

"There are but two sorts of men in the world, freemen and slaves. The very definition of a freeman is one who is bound by no law to which he has not consented."[136] (Note: John and Abigail were deeply opposed to slavery) - John Adams

On American Greatness:

"I know America capable of anything she undertakes with spirit and vigor."[137] - Abigail Adams

On Equality:

"And, by the way, in the new code of laws which I suppose it will be necessary for you to make, I desire you would remember the ladies and be more generous and favorable to them than your ancestors."[138] - Abigail Adams

Against Slavery:

"It always appeared a most iniquitous scheme to me - to fight ourselves for what we are daily robbing and plundering from those who have as good a right to freedom as we have."[139] John Adams

---

[135] John Adams "Novanglus Essays" in John Adams, Works, (The Perfect Library), (Amazon Kindle), Kindle Location 71 percent of 100.

[136] John Adams "Novanglus Essays" in John Adams, Works, (The Perfect Library), (Amazon Kindle), Kindle Location 16 percent of 100.

[137] Abigail Adams "Letter to John" in Familiar Letters of John Adams and His Wife Abigail Adams During the Revolution, ed. Charles Francis Adams (New York: Hurd and Houghton, 1875). A Public Domain Book, (Amazon Kindle), Kindle Location 93 percent of 100.

[138] Abigail Adams "Letter to John" in Familiar Letters of John Adams and His Wife Abigail Adams During the Revolution, ed. Charles Francis Adams (New York: Hurd and Houghton, 1875). A Public Domain Book, (Amazon Kindle), Kindle Location 93 percent of 100.

[139] John Adams "Letter to Abigail" in Familiar Letters of John Adams and His Wife Abigail Adams During the Revolution, ed. Charles Francis Adams (New York: Hurd and Houghton, 1875). A Public Domain Book, (Amazon Kindle), Kindle Location 15 percent of 100.

Alexis de Toqueville, Quotes for Conservatives and Republicans

Alexis de Toqueville wrote one of the first, and certainly the most famous, works of political science about the United States. His two-volume work, *Democracy in America*, offers by far the best and most comprehensive view of what the America that the founding fathers bequeathed to their children looked like.

Himself a Frenchman, Toqueville had little stake in American political decision-making. He merely reported on the American condition (in the early 1830s) as he saw it. What he saw was an America whose beliefs modern conservatives and Republicans would recognize as closely matching their own.

Toqueville saw an America where every backwoods farmer kept and read, not only a copy of the Bible, but often numerous classical works. That same America, he reported, saw the Christian religion as the basis for its political ideas. It disdained intrusive government, preferred local decision-making, declined to alter the Constitution to suit the needs of either political party, and was eager to take advantage of the enormous opportunity afforded it by a material-rich continent.

Many of Toqueville's most important observations on America are quoted in the pages that follow.

Religion, Morals, Civil Society and Their Effect on Government:

"...in America religion is the road to knowledge, and the observance of the divine laws leads man to civil freedom."[140] - Alexis de Toqueville

"It was never assumed in the United States that the citizen of a free country has a right to do whatever he pleases; on the contrary, social obligations were there imposed upon him more various than anywhere else."[141] - Alexis de Toqueville

"The safeguard of morality is religion, and morality is the best security of law and the surest pledge of freedom."[142] - Alexis de Toqueville

"The Americans combine the notions of Christianity and of liberty so intimately in their minds, that it is impossible to make them conceive the one without the other."[143] - Alexis de Toqueville

"There is no country in the world in which everything can be provided for by the laws, or in which political institutions can prove a substitute for common sense and public morality. p.98

"A false notion which is clear and precise will always meet with a greater number of adherents in the world than a true principle which is obscure or involved."[144] - Alexis de Toqueville

---

[140] Toqueville, Democracy in America: Volume I. P. 24
[141] Toqueville, Democracy in America: Volume I. P. 50
[142] Toqueville, Democracy in America: Volume I. P. 26
[143] Toqueville, Democracy in America: Volume I. P. 272

"...[F]rom the earliest settlement of the emigrants politics and religion contracted an alliance which has never been dissolved."[145] - Alexis de Toqueville

"I am convinced that the most advantageous situation and the best possible laws cannot maintain a constitution in spite of the manners [morals] of a country; whilst the latter may turn the most unfavorable positions and the worst laws to some advantage."[146] - Alexis de Toqueville

"In the nations by which the sovereignty of the people is recognized every individual possesses an equal share of power, and participates alike in the government of the State. Every individual is, therefore, supposed to be as well informed, as virtuous and as strong as any of his fellow citizens."[147] - Alexis de Toqueville

"...[T]he Puritans went forth to seek some rude and unfrequented part of the world, where they could live according to their own opinions, and worship God in freedom."[148] - Alexis de Toqueville

"It must not be imagined that the piety of the Puritans was of a merely speculative kind, or that it took no cognizance of the course of worldly affairs. Puritanism, as I have already remarked, was scarcely less a political than a religious doctrine." - Alexis de Toqueville, 1835, Democracy in America p.15

"A certain uniformity of civilization is not less necessary to the durability of a confederation than a uniformity of interests in the States which compose it."[149] - Alexis de Toqueville

"Both parties of the Americans were, in fact, agreed upon the most essential points; and neither of them had to destroy a traditionary constitution, or to overthrow the structure of society, in order to ensure its own triumph."[150] - Alexis de Toqueville

"There is certainly no country in the world where the tie of marriage is so much respected as in America, or where conjugal happiness is more highly or worthily appreciated. In Europe almost all the disturbances of society arise from the irregularities of domestic life."[151] - Alexis de Toqueville

"The idea of right is simply that of virtue introduced into the political world."[152] - Alexis de Toqueville

"How is it possible that society should escape destruction if the moral tie be not strengthened in proportion as the political tie is relaxed?"[153] - Alexis de Toqueville

---

[144] Toqueville, Democracy in America: Volume I. P. 183
[145] Toqueville, Democracy in America: Volume I. P. 266
[146] Toqueville, Democracy in America: Volume I. P. 287
[147] Toqueville, Democracy in America: Volume I. P. 244
[148] Toqueville, Democracy in America: Volume I. P. 14
[149] Toqueville, Democracy in America: Volume I. P. 142
[150] Toqueville, Democracy in America: Volume I. P. 148
[151] Toqueville, Democracy in America: Volume I. P. 270
[152] Toqueville, Democracy in America: Volume I. P. 214
[153] Toqueville, Democracy in America: Volume I. P. 273

"Unlimited power is in itself a bad and dangerous thing; human beings are not competent to exercise it with discretion, and God alone can be omnipotent, because His wisdom and His justice are always equal to His power."[154] - Alexis de Toqueville

"In New England the same magistrates are empowered to post the names of habitual drunkards in public-houses, and to prohibit the inhabitants of a town from supplying them with liquor. A censorial power of this excessive kind would be revolting to the population of the most absolute monarchies; here, however, it is submitted to without difficulty."[155] - Alexis de Toqueville

"Despotism may govern without faith, but liberty cannot."[156] - Alexis de Toqueville

"It may be asserted that in the United States no religious doctrine displays the slightest hostility to democratic and republican institutions."[157] - Alexis de Toqueville

"Upon my arrival in the United States, the religious aspect of the country was the first thing that struck my attention; and the longer I stayed there the more did I perceive the great political consequences resulting from this state of things, to which I was unaccustomed."[158] - Alexis de Toqueville

"I have just shown what the direct influence of religion upon politics is in the United States, but its indirect influence appears to me to be still more considerable, and it never instructs the Americans more fully in the art of being free than when it says nothing of freedom."[159] - Alexis de Toqueville

"Moreover, almost all the sects of the United States are comprised within the great unity of Christianity, and Christian morality is everywhere the same."[160] - Alexis de Toqueville

"Lord, turn not Thou Thy face from us, and grant that we may always be the most religious as well as the freest people of the Earth."[161] - A priest, as quoted by Alexis de Toqueville

"...[B]ut there is no country in the whole world in which the Christian religion retains a greater influence over the souls of men than in America; and there can be no greater proof of its utility, and of its conformity to human nature, than that its influence is most powerfully felt over the most enlightened and free nation of the earth."[162] - Alexis de Toqueville

"Although the Anglo-Americans have several religious sects, they all regard religion in the same manner...they are unanimous upon the general principles which ought to rule human society."[163] - Alexis de Toqueville

---

[154] Toqueville, Democracy in America: Volume I. P. 229
[155] Toqueville, Democracy in America: Volume I. P. 180
[156] Toqueville, Democracy in America: Volume I. P. 273
[157] Toqueville, Democracy in America: Volume I. P. 268
[158] Toqueville, Democracy in America: Volume I. P. 274
[159] Toqueville, Democracy in America: Volume I. P. 269
[160] Ibid.
[161] A Priest Quoted by Alexis de Toqueville, in Democracy in America, by Alexis de Toqueville (IndyPublish), p. 269.
[162] Toqueville, Democracy in America: Volume I. P. 270
[163] Toqueville, Democracy in America: Volume I. P. 354

"That providence has given to every human being the degree of reason necessary to direct himself in the affairs which interest him exclusively - such is the grand maxim upon which civil and political society rests in the United States."[164] - Alexis de Toqueville

"It is difficult to imagine the incredible rapidity with which public opinion circulates in the midst of these deserts. I do not think so much intellectual intercourse takes place in the most enlightened and populous districts of France."[165] - Alexis de Toqueville

"Physical causes do not, therefore, affect the destiny of nations so much as has been supposed."[166] - Alexis de Toqueville

Economics and American Enterprise:

"It seemed as if New England was a region given up to the dreams of fancy and the unrestrained experiments of innovators."[167] - Alexis de Toqueville

"I do not mean that there is any deficiency of wealthy individuals in the United States; I know of no country, indeed, where the love of money has taken stronger hold on the affections of men, and where the profounder contempt is expressed for the theory of the permanent equality of property. But wealth circulates with inconceivable rapidity, and experience shows that it is rare to find two succeeding generations [in America] in the full enjoyment of it."[168] - Alexis de Toqueville

"In general the American system is not to grant fixed salary to its functionaries. Every service has its price, and they are remunerated in proportion to what they have done."[169] - Alexis de Toqueville

The Americans frequently term what we should call cupidity a laudable industry; and they blame as faint-heartedness what we consider to be the virtue of moderate desires."[170] - Alexis de Toqueville

"When a private individual [in America] meditates an undertaking, however directly connected it may be with the welfare of society, he never thinks of soliciting the co-operation of the Government, but he publishes his plan, offers to execute it himself, courts the assistance of other individuals, and struggles manfully against all obstacles."[171] - Alexis de Toqueville

"The citizen of the United States is taught from his earliest infancy to rely upon his own exertions in order to resist the evils and the difficulties of life; he looks upon social authority with an eye of mistrust and anxiety, and he only claims its assistance when he is quite unable to shift without it."[172] - Alexis de Toqueville

---

[164] Toqueville, Democracy in America: Volume I. P. 387
[165] Toqueville, Democracy in America: Volume I. P. 282
[166] Toqueville, Democracy in America: Volume I. P. 285
[167] Toqueville, Democracy in America: Volume I. P. 18
[168] Toqueville, Democracy in America: Volume I. P. 33
[169] Toqueville, Democracy in America: Volume I. P. 44
[170] Toqueville, Democracy in America: Volume I. P. 263
[171] Toqueville, Democracy in America: Volume I. P. 72
[172] Toqueville, Democracy in America: Volume I. P. 162

"If a stoppage occurs in a thoroughfare, and the circulation of the public is hindered, the neighbors immediately constitute a deliberative body; and this extemporaneous assembly gives rise to an execution of power which remedies the inconvenience before anybody has thought of recurring to an authority superior to that of the persons immediately concerned."[173] - Alexis de Toqueville

"At the present time America presents a field for human effort far more extensive than any sum of labor which can be applied to work it."[174] - Alexis de Toqueville

"In America those complaints against property in general which are so frequent in Europe are never heard, because in America there are no paupers; and as everyone has property of his own to defend, everyone recognizes the principle upon which he holds it."[175] - Alexis de Toqueville

"It is certain that despotism ruins individuals by preventing them from producing wealth, much more than by depriving them of the wealth they have produced; it dries up the source of riches, whilst it usually respects acquired property. Freedom, on the contrary, engenders far more benefits than it destroys; and the nations which are favored by free institutions invariably find that their resources increase even more rapidly than their taxes."[176] - Alexis de Toqueville

"...[T]here is no public indigence to supply the means of agitation, because the physical position of the country opens so wide a field to industry that man is able to accomplish the most surprising undertakings with his own native resources."[177] - Alexis de Toqueville

"It is so easy to acquire an independent position in the United States that the public officer who loses his place may be deprived of the comforts of life, but not of the means of subsistence."[178] - Alexis de Toqueville

"It is difficult to describe the rapacity with which the American rushes forward to secure the immense booty which fortune proffers to him."[179] - Alexis de Toqueville

Limited Government, Federalism and Local Authority:

"In the estimation of the democracy a government is not a benefit, but a necessary evil."[180] - Alexis de Toqueville

"The political existence of the majority of the nations of Europe commenced in the superior ranks of society, and was gradually and imperfectly communicated to the different members of the social body. In America...it may be said that the township was organized before the county, the county before the State, the State before the Union."[181] - Alexis de Toqueville

---

[173] Toqueville, Democracy in America: Volume I. P. 163
[174] Toqueville, Democracy in America: Volume I. P. 263
[175] Toqueville, Democracy in America: Volume I. P. 215
[176] Toqueville, Democracy in America: Volume I. P. 183
[177] Toqueville, Democracy in America: Volume I. P. 150
[178] Toqueville, Democracy in America: Volume I. P. 106
[179] Toqueville, Democracy in America: Volume I. P. 261
[180] Toqueville, Democracy in America: Volume I. P. 177
[181] Toqueville, Democracy in America: Volume I. P. 23

"Whenever the political laws of the United States are to be discussed, it is with the doctrine of the sovereignty of the people that we must begin."[182] - Alexis de Toqueville

"Moreover, the Federal Government is, as I have just observed, the exception; the Government of the States is the rule."[183] - Alexis de Toqueville

"In the laws of Connecticut, as well as in all those of New England, we find the germ and gradual development of that township independence which is the life and mainspring of American liberty at the present day."[184] - Alexis de Toqueville

"Nevertheless local assemblies of citizens constitute the strength of free nations."[185] - Alexis de Toqueville

"It profits me but little, after all, that a vigilant authority should...constantly avert all dangers from my path...if this same authority is the absolute mistress of my liberty..."[186] - Alexis de Toqueville
"Hitherto no one in the United States has dared to advance the maxim, that everything is permissible with a view to the interests of society; an impious adage which seems to have been invented in an age of freedom to shelter all the tyrants of future ages."[187] - Alexis de Toqueville

"The powers delegated by the Constitution to the Federal Government are few and defined. Those which are to remain in the State governments are numerous and indefinite. The former will be exercised principally on external objects, as war, peace, negotiation and foreign commerce. The powers reserved to the several States will extend to all the objects which, in the ordinary course...concern the internal order and prosperity of the state."[188] Alexis de Toqueville

"The Europeans believe that liberty is promoted by depriving the social authority of some of its rights; the Americans, by dividing its exercise."[189] - Alexis de Toqueville

"No idea was ever entertained [in America] of attacking the principles or of contesting the rights of society; but the exercise of its authority was divided, to the end that the office might be powerful and the officer insignificant...."[190] - Alexis de Toqueville

"However enlightened and however skillful a central power may be, it cannot of itself embrace all the details of the existence of a great nation."[191] - Alexis de Toqueville

"In America the President cannot prevent any law from being passed, nor can he evade the obligation of enforcing it."[192] - Alexis de Toqueville

---

[182] Toqueville, Democracy in America: Volume I. P. 36
[183] Toqueville, Democracy in America: Volume I. P. 39
[184] Toqueville, Democracy in America: Volume I. P. 23
[185] Toqueville, Democracy in America: Volume I. P. 41
[186] Toqueville, Democracy in America: Volume I. P. 70
[187] Toqueville, Democracy in America: Volume I. P. 271
[188] James Madison, "The Federalist No. 45" in Democracy in America, by Alexis de Toqueville (IndyPublish), p. 91.
[189] Toqueville, Democracy in America: Volume I. P. 49
[190] Toqueville, Democracy in America: Volume I. P. 50
[191] Toqueville, Democracy in America: Volume I. P. 68
[192] Toqueville, Democracy in America: Volume I. P. 103

"On the other hand, when a republic falls under the sway of a single individual, the demeanor of the sovereign is simple and unpretending, as if his authority was not yet paramount."[193] - Alexis de Toqueville

"A constitutional King in Europe is not merely the executor of the law, but the execution of its provisions devolves so completely upon him that he has the power of paralyzing its influence if it opposes his designs."[194] - Alexis de Toqueville

"In the United States the action of the Government may be slackened with impunity, because it is always weak and circumscribed."[195] - Alexis de Toqueville

"It is incontestably true that the love and the habits of republican government in the United States were engendered in the townships and in the provincial assemblies."[196] - Alexis de Toqueville

"In France the State-collector receives the local imposts; in America the town-collector receives the taxes of the State."[197] - Alexis de Toqueville

"The Americans have a federal and the French a national Government."[198] - Alexis de Toqueville

"Nothing is more striking to a European traveler in the United States than the absence of what we term the Government, or the Administration."[199] - Alexis de Toqueville

"In America the public acts of a community frequently leave fewer traces than the occurrences of a family."[200] - Alexis de Toqueville

"The first is common in the United States, but not the second: the Americans often change their laws, but the foundation of the Constitution is respected."[201] - Alexis de Toqueville

"In no country in the world does the law hold so absolute a language as in America, and in no country is the right of applying it vested in so many hands."[202] - Alexis de Toqueville

"I am persuaded, on the contrary, that in this case [of America] the collective strength of the citizens will always conduce more efficaciously to the public welfare than the authority of the government."[203] - Alexis de Toqueville

"On my arrival in the United States I was surprised to find so much distinguished talent among the subjects, and so little among the heads of the Government."[204] - Alexis de Toqueville

---

[193] Toqueville, Democracy in America: Volume I. P. 99
[194] Toqueville, Democracy in America: Volume I. P. 102
[195] Toqueville, Democracy in America: Volume I. P. 105
[196] Toqueville, Democracy in America: Volume I. P. 136
[197] Toqueville, Democracy in America: Volume I. P. 45
[198] Toqueville, Democracy in America: Volume I. P. 99
[199] Toqueville, Democracy in America: Volume I. P. 49
[200] Toqueville, Democracy in America: Volume I. P. 181
[201] Toqueville, Democracy in America: Volume I. P. 388
[202] Toqueville, Democracy in America: Volume I. P. 50
[203] Toqueville, Democracy in America: Volume I. P. 68

"It was indispensable to the maintenance of the republican form of government that the representative of the executive power [the president] should be subject to the will of the nation."[205] – Alexis de Toqueville

"If a stoppage occurs in a thoroughfare, and the circulation of the public is hindered, the neighbors immediately constitute a deliberative body; and this extemporaneous assembly gives rise to an execution of power which remedies the inconvenience before anybody has thought of recurring to an authority superior to that of the persons immediately concerned."[206] - Alexis de Toqueville

"Public officers in the United States are commingled with the crowd of citizens; they have neither palaces, nor guards, nor ceremonial costumes."[207] - Alexis de Toqueville

"In the United States the persons who engage in the perplexities of political life are individuals of very moderate pretensions. The pursuit of wealth generally diverts men of great talents and of great passion from the pursuit of power, and it very frequently happens that a man does not undertake to direct the fortune of the State until he has discovered his incompetence to conduct his own affairs."[208] - Alexis de Toqueville

Democracy and Freedom:

"How can a populace, unaccustomed to freedom in small concerns, learn to use it temperately in great affairs? What resistance can be offered to tyranny in a country where every private individual is impotent, and where citizens are united by no common tie?"[209] - Alexis de Toqueville

"There is, in fact, a manly and lawful passion for equality which excites men to wish all to be powerful and honored. This passion tends to elevate the humble to the rank of the great; but there exists also in the human heart a depraved taste for equality, which impels the weak to attempt to lower the powerful to their own level, and reduces men to prefer equality in slavery to inequality with freedom."[210] - Alexis de Toqueville

"The English colonies (and this is one of the main causes of their prosperity) have always enjoyed more internal freedom and more political independence than the colonies of other nations..."[211] - Alexis de Toqueville

"...whilst political laws are only the symbol of a nation's condition, they exercise an incredible influence upon its social state."[212] - Alexis de Toqueville

---

[204] Toqueville, Democracy in America: Volume I. P. 171
[205] Toqueville, Democracy in America: Volume I. P. 97
[206] Toqueville, Democracy in America: Volume I. P. 163
[207] Toqueville, Democracy in America: Volume I. P. 177
[208] Toqueville, Democracy in America: Volume I. P. 179
[209] Toqueville, Democracy in America: Volume I. P. 73
[210] Toqueville, Democracy in America: Volume I. P. 35
[211] Toqueville, Democracy in America: Volume I. P. 18
[212] Toqueville, Democracy in America: Volume I. P. 29

"It is incontestable that in times of danger a free people displays far more energy than one which is not so."[213] - Alexis de Toqueville

"Physical strength is therefore one of the first conditions of the happiness and even of the existence of nations."[214] - Alexis de Toqueville

"The Republican principle demands that the deliberative sense of the community should govern the conduct of those to whom they entrust the management of their affairs; but it does not require an unqualified complaisance to every sudden breeze of passion, or to every transient impulse which the people may receive from the arts of men who flatter their prejudices to betray their interests."[215] - Alexis de Toqueville

"In America there is scarcely a hamlet which has not its own newspaper."[216] - Alexis de Toqueville

"The United States afford[s] the first example of the kind."[217] - Alexis de Toqueville

"This is frequently true, although a democracy is more liable to error than a monarch or a body of nobles; the chances of its regaining the right path when once it has acknowledged its mistake, are greater also; because it is rarely embarrassed by internal interests, which conflict with those of the majority, and resist the authority of reason."[218] - Alexis de Toqueville

"There is more calculation, even in the impulses of bravery, than is generally attributed to them; and although the first efforts are suggested by passion, perseverance is maintained by a distinct regard of the purpose in view."[219] - Alexis de Toqueville

"I am of opinion that a democratic government tends in the end to increase the real strength of society..."[220] - Alexis de Toqueville

"The great privilege of the Americans does not simply consist in their being more enlightened than other nations, but in their being able to repair the faults they may commit."[221] - Alexis de Toqueville

"...[D]espotism often promises to make amends for a thousand previous ills; it supports the right, it protects the oppressed, and it maintains public order. The nation is lulled by the temporary prosperity which accrues to it, until it is roused to a sense of its own misery."[222] - Alexis de Toqueville

---

[213] Toqueville, Democracy in America: Volume I. P. 199
[214] Toqueville, Democracy in America: Volume I. P. 135
[215] Toqueville, Democracy in America: Volume I. P. 127
[216] Toqueville, Democracy in America: Volume I. P. 158
[217] Toqueville, Democracy in America: Volume I. P. 198
[218] Toqueville, Democracy in America: Volume I. P. 201
[219] Toqueville, Democracy in America: Volume I. P. 199
[220] Toqueville, Democracy in America: Volume I. P. 200
[221] Toqueville, Democracy in America: Volume I. P. 201
[222] Toqueville, Democracy in America: Volume I. P. 216

"In our times option must be made between the patriotism of all and the government of a few; for the force and activity which the first confers are irreconcilable with the guarantees of tranquility which the second furnishes."[223] - Alexis de Toqueville

"But I do not think that a democratic power is naturally without force or without resources: say, rather, that it is almost always by the abuse of its force and the misemployment of its resources that a democratic government fails."[224] - Alexis de Toqueville

The Supreme Court and the Judiciary:

"The peace, the prosperity, and the very existence of the Union are vested in the hands of the seven [now nine] judges. Without their active co-operation the Constitution would be a dead letter."[225] - Alexis de Toqueville

"But it is better to grant the power of changing the constitution of the people to men who represent (however imperfectly) to will of the people, than to men who represent no one but themselves."[226] - Alexis de Toqueville

"Both parties of the Americans were, in fact, agreed upon the most essential points; and neither of them had to destroy a traditionary constitution, or to overthrow the structure of society, in order to ensure its own triumph."[227] - Alexis de Toqueville

"The authority which is awarded to the intervention of a court of justice by the general opinion of mankind is so surprisingly great that it clings to the mere formalities of justice, and gives a bodily influence to the shadow of the law."[228] - Alexis de Toqueville

"But this is not always the case in countries in which the sovereignty is divided; in [others] the judicial power is more frequently opposed to a fraction of the nation than to an isolated individual, and its moral authority and physical strength are consequently diminished."[229] - Alexis de Toqueville

"When we have successively examined in detail the organization of the Supreme Court, and the entire prerogatives which it exercises, we shall readily admit that a more imposing judicial power was never constituted by any people."[230] - Alexis de Toqueville

"The tranquility and the very existence of the Union depend on the discretion of the seven [now nine] Federal Judges."[231] - Alexis de Toqueville

"But if the Supreme Court is ever composed of imprudent men or bad citizens, the Union may be plunged into anarchy..."[232] - Alexis de Toqueville

---

[223] Toqueville, Democracy in America: Volume I. P. 214
[224] Toqueville, Democracy in America: Volume I. P. 237
[225] Toqueville, Democracy in America: Volume I. P. 125
[226] Toqueville, Democracy in America: Volume I. P. 78
[227] Toqueville, Democracy in America: Volume I. P. 148
[228] Toqueville, Democracy in America: Volume I. P. 114
[229] Toqueville, Democracy in America: Volume I. P. 122
[230] Toqueville, Democracy in America: Volume I. P. 124
[231] Toqueville, Democracy in America: Volume I. P. 124

On American Exceptionalism:

"To evils which are common to all democratic peoples they have applied remedies which none but themselves had ever thought of before; and although they were the first to make the experiment, they have succeeded in it."[233] - Alexis de Toqueville

On Slavery:

"God forbid that I should seek to justify the principle of...slavery, as has been done by some American writers!"[234] - Alexis de Toqueville

Thoughts on Future Global Power:

"The Anglo-American relies upon personal interest to accomplish his ends, and gives free scope to the unguided exertions and common-sense of the citizens; the Russian centres all the authority of society in a single arm; the principle instrument of the former is freedom; of the latter servitude. Their starting - point is different, and their courses are not the same; yet each of them seems to be marked out by the will of Heaven to sway the destinies of half the globe."[235]
- Alexis de Toqueville

[232] Toqueville, Democracy in America: Volume I. P. 126
[233] Toqueville, Democracy in America: Volume I. P. 289
[234] Toqueville, Democracy in America: Volume I. P. 340
[235] Toqueville, Democracy in America: Volume I. P. Conclusion

Thomas Paine, Quotes for Conservatives and Republicans

The following quotes are a compendium of ideas taken from Thomas Paine's *Common Sense* pamphlet. No single piece of writing did more to stir the American colonists to fight for independence. Almost as important, it helped to shape George Washington's thoughts on liberty.

The pamphlet immediately sold hundreds of thousands of copies – no small feat, given that the population of the colonies at the time was around 2.5 million.

Paine was close to many of our other founding fathers, including Benjamin Franklin. His ideas are reproduced here for their support of limited government, religious liberty, and limited national borrowing. These ideas are shared by modern conservatives.

It is important to note that in a later publication, which was criticized roundly by John Adams, Samuel Adams, Patrick Henry, and John Jay, as well as privately by Benjamin Franklin, Paine professed a disdain for religion. Franklin in particular warned Paine that no good could come of depriving the populace of a primary motive for acting justly. Thus, Paine eventually broke with what we now consider to be conservative ideology, as expressed by the likes of Ronald Reagan,[236] (although conservatives do and should support religious freedom) but his sentiments in Common Sense otherwise offer a good source of inspiration.

On Limited Government:

"Society in every state is a blessing, but government, even in its best state, is but a necessary evil..."[237] - Thomas Paine

"I draw my idea of the form of government from a principle in nature, which no art can overturn, viz. that the more simple any thing is, the less liable it is to be disordered; and the easier repaired when disordered..."[238] - Thomas Paine

"Some writers have so confounded society with government, as to leave little or no distinction between them; whereas they are not only different, but have different origins. Society is produced by our wants, and government by our wickedness...The first is a patron, the last is a punisher."[239] - Thomas Paine

"Of more worth is one honest man to society, and in the sight of God, than all the crowned ruffians that ever lived."[240] - Thomas Paine

"The state of a king shuts him from the world, yet the business of a king requires him to know it thoroughly..."[241] - Thomas Paine

---

[236] Coulter, Treason. pp. 164-166

[237] Paine, Common Sense. p. 1

[238] Paine, Common Sense. p. 4

[239] Paine, Common Sense. p. 1

[240] Paine, Common Sense. p. 20

"How came the king by a power which the people are afraid to trust, and always obliged to check?"[242] - Thomas Paine

"Near three thousand years passed away from the Mosaic account of the creation, till the Jews, under a national delusion, requested a king."[243] - Thomas Paine

On Money and Finances:

"Wherefore, security being the true design and end of government, it unanswerably follows that whatever form thereof appears most likely to ensure it to us, with the least expence and greatest benefit, is prefarable to all others."[244] - Thomas Paine

"Our plan is commerce, and that, well attended to, will secure us the peace and friendship of all Europe..."[245] - Thomas Paine

"As parents, we can have no joy, knowing that this government is not sufficiently lasting to ensure any thing which we may bequeath to posterity; and by a plain method of argument, as we are running the next generation into debt, we ought to do the work of it, otherwise we use them meanly and pitifully."[246] - Thomas Paine

On a Separate Political Class:

"...and that the *elected* might never form to themselves an interest separate from the *electors*, prudence will point out the propriety of having elections often: because as the *elected* might by that means return and mix again with the general body of the *electors*, in a few months, their fidelity to the public will be secured by the prudent reflection of not making a rod for themselves."[247] - Thomas Paine

On Religious Liberty:

"This new world hath been the asylum for the persecuted lovers of civil and religious liberty from *every part* of Europe."[248] - Thomas Paine

On National Defense:

"In point of safety, ought we to be without a fleet? We are not the little people now, which we were sixty years ago; at that time we might have trusted our property in the streets, or fields rather; and slept securely without locks or bolts to our doors or windows. The case is now

---

[241] Paine, Common Sense. p. 6
[242] Paine, Common Sense. p. 7
[243] Paine, Common Sense. p. 10
[244] Paine, Common Sense. p. 2
[245] Paine, Common Sense. p. 26
[246] Paine, Common Sense. p. 26
[247] Paine, Common Sense. p. 4
[248] Paine, Common Sense. p. 24

altered, and our methods of defence ought to improve with our increase of property."[249] - Thomas Paine

"To unite the sinews of commerce and defense is sound policy; for when our strength and our riches play into each other's hands, we need fear no external enemy."[250] - Thomas Paine

---

[249] Paine, Common Sense. p. 24

[250] Paine, Common Sense. pp. 49-50

Benjamin Franklin Quotes for Conservatives and Republicans

Dr. Benjamin Franklin's role in American history can hardly be overstated.

He was, by far, the most prominent colonist in the years leading up to America's revolutionary war.[251]

He published his own newspaper, the Pennsylvania Gazette – the most successful paper in the colonies.[252] His books and articles, sometimes published under pen names, were famous. He was also a great inventor, having invented, among other things, the lightning rod, a device that saved innumerable lives from the dangers of fire.

In 1753, he was appointed Britain's postmaster general of the colonies. While still postmaster, he acted as Pennsylvania's – and later the colonies' – representative in London, in the period leading up to the revolution. While there, his British hosts attempted to humiliate him[253] during a hearing of the Privy Council, essentially accusing him of treason. While such an accusation could have placed Franklin in a great deal of personal danger, he suffered nothing worse than the loss of his postmaster position two days later, and was soon named postmaster again – this time by the Continental Congress.

Upon returning to America, Franklin took up the cause of independence in full, having seen for himself how unlikely a compromise between Britain and America was. He represented Pennsylvania as a delegate to the Second Continental Congress, served on the committee that wrote the Declaration of Independence, and signed the declaration along with fifty-four others. His signature appears to the right of John Hancock's, and just below that of Benjamin Rush.

During the war, he served with great success as America's ambassador to France. He was vital to the American effort to secure French money for the revolutionary cause. Eventually, he was able to secure full military aid from France as well – the one nation whose power rivaled Britain's on the world stage. Without that aid, the outcome of the war would likely have been far less favorable to his fledgling country, even if only in terms of the length of conflict, and the rights and territories the United States was able to secure when the dust finally settled.

After it was all over, Franklin signed the Treaty of Paris on behalf of the American people, in which Britain recognized the fait accompli of American independence.

A few years later, he would add yet another laurel to his career by serving as a delegate to the Constitutional Convention, which created a charter for his new nation that remains in effect to this day.

His other accomplishments are so numerous that a separate book would be required to even briefly discuss them.

---

[251] Brands, The First American. p. 444

[252] The Pennsylvania Gazette. Accessible Archives. Accessed 1/10/18. http://www.accessible-archives.com/collections/the-pennsylvania-gazette/

[253] Brands, The First American. p. 1

The following quotes illustrate his ideas.

On Economics and Enterprise:

"There are no gains without pains."[254] - Benjamin Franklin

"At the working man's house hunger looks in but dares not enter."[255] - Benjamin Franklin

"Beware of little expenses, a small leak will sink a great ship."[256] - Benjamin Franklin

"Diligence is the mother of good luck."[257] - Benjamin Franklin

On Self and National Defense:

"Love your neighbor Yet don't pull down your hedge."[258] - Benjamin Franklin

"The wolf sheds his coat once a year, his disposition never."[259] - Benjamin Franklin

"Beware of meat twice boiled And of an old foe reconciled."[260] - Benjamin Franklin

"Many Foxes grow grey, but few grow good."[261] - Benjamin Franklin

On Limited Government:

"The king's cheese is half wasted in parings; but no matter, 'tis made of the people's milk."[262] - Benjamin Franklin

"Kings have long arms, but Misfortune longer, Let none think themselves out of her reach."[263] - Benjamin Franklin

"In rivers and bad governments the lightest things swim to the top."[264] - Benjamin Franklin

Religion, Morals, Civil Society, and Their Effect on Government:

"Fear God, and your Enemies will fear you."[265] - Benjamin Franklin

---

[254] Franklin, Poor Richard's Almanac. Kindle Location 4 percent of 100
[255] Ibid.
[256] Franklin, Poor Richard's Almanac. Kindle Location 28 percent of 100
[257] Franklin, Poor Richard's Almanac. Kindle Location 4 percent of 100
[258] Franklin, Poor Richard's Almanac. Kindle Location 17 percent of 100
[259] Franklin, Poor Richard's Almanac. Kindle Location 40 percent of 100
[260] Franklin, Poor Richard's Almanac. Kindle Location 33 percent of 100
[261] Franklin, Poor Richard's Almanac. Kindle Location 45 percent of 100
[262] Franklin, Poor Richard's Almanac. Kindle Location 46 percent of 100
[263] Franklin, Poor Richard's Almanac. Kindle Location 27 percent of 100
[264] Franklin, Poor Richard's Almanac. Kindle Location 61 percent of 100
[265] Franklin, Poor Richard's Almanac. Kindle Location 89 percent of 100

"No longer virtuous no longer free; is a Maxim as true with regard to a private Person as a Common-wealth."[266] - Benjamin Franklin

"Sell not virtue to purchase wealth nor liberty to purchase power."[267] - Benjamin Franklin

"Nothing brings more pain than too much pleasure; nothing more bondage than too much liberty."[268] - Benjamin Franklin

"Virtue and a trade are a child's best portion."[269] - Benjamin Franklin

O! 'tis easier to keep holiday's than commandments."[270] - Benjamin Franklin

"Sin is not hurtful because it is forbidden but it is forbidden because it's hurtful."[271] - Benjamin Franklin

"Virtue and happiness are mother and daughter."[272] - Benjamin Franklin

"The proud hate pride - in others."[273] - Benjamin Franklin

"The noblest question in the world is What good may I do in it?"[274] - Benjamin Franklin

On Intellectual Pursuits:

"A learned blockhead is a greater blockhead than an ignorant one."[275] - Benjamin Franklin

"The learned fool writes his nonsense in better language than the unlearned; but it is still nonsense."[276] - Benjamin Franklin

"Historians relate, not so much what is done, as what they would have believed."[277] - Benjamin Franklin

"Blame-all and Praise-all are two blockheads."[278] - Benjamin Franklin

"He that composes himself is wiser than he that composes books."[279] - Benjamin Franklin

---

[266] Franklin, Poor Richard's Almanac. Kindle Location 78 percent of 100
[267] Franklin, Poor Richard's Almanac. Kindle Location 13 percent of 100
[268] Ibid.
[269] Franklin, Poor Richard's Almanac. Kindle Location 17 percent of 100
[270] Franklin, Poor Richard's Almanac. Kindle Location 46 percent of 100
[271] Franklin, Poor Richard's Almanac. Kindle Location 79 percent of 100
[272] Franklin, Poor Richard's Almanac. Kindle Location 65 percent of 100
[273] Franklin, Poor Richard's Almanac. Kindle Location 10 percent of 100
[274] Franklin, Poor Richard's Almanac. Kindle Location 13 percent of 100
[275] Franklin, Poor Richard's Almanac. Kindle Location 12 percent of 100
[276] Ibid.
[277] Franklin, Poor Richard's Almanac. Kindle Location 76 percent of 100
[278] Franklin, Poor Richard's Almanac. Kindle Location 11 percent of 100
[279] Franklin, Poor Richard's Almanac. Kindle Location 35 percent of 100

John Locke, Quotes for Conservatives and Republicans

The following quotes are a compendium of ideas and observations from John Locke's *Second Treatise of Government*, which many historians and scholars view as his most important work.

Locke was one of the most renowned political thinkers of the Enlightenment. His influence on the thinking of America's early leaders was profound.

As Locke himself was from the country they were breaking away from, as well as a political theorist in what we would now think of as the conservative mold, his ideas helped give America's founding fathers a solid intellectual basis for their revolution. Locke provided the outline for the Declaration of Independence's inalienable rights of man (life, liberty, and the pursuit of happiness) with his belief in "life, liberty, and property". He also contributed greatly to a discussion that was ongoing then as now – specifically, concerning what defines the "laws of nature".

Locke also advocated for ideas that most Americans today would recognize – that no one should be above the law, that no one's property can be taken away without their consent, and that it is dangerous to have a political class that is separate from or above the people.

As Locke's ideas are so vital to understanding the views of America's founding fathers, and formed the basis for much of their thinking, they are faithfully reproduced below, especially where they relate to modern conservative thought.

Some of the following quotes are also rather long, as Locke's generation did not place great deal of emphasis on punctuation.

Religious Faith as the Reasoning for Free Government and Law:

"Thus the law of nature stands as an eternal rule to all men, legislators as well as others. The rules that they make for other men's actions, must, as well as their own and other men's actions, be conformable to the law of nature, i.e. to the will of God, of which that is a declaration, and the fundamental law of nature being the preservation of mankind, no human sanction can be good, or valid against it."[280] - John Locke

"The state of nature has a law of nature to govern it, which obliges every one: and reason, which is that law, teaches all mankind, who will but consult it, that being all equal and independent, no one ought to harm another in his life, liberty, or possession, for men being all the workmanship of one omnipotent, and infinitely wise maker..."[281] - John Locke

"In transgressing the law of Nature, the offender declares himself to live by another rule than that of reason and common equality, which is that measure God has set to the actions of men, for their mutual security; and so he becomes dangerous to mankind, the tye, which is to secure them from injury and violence, being slighted and broken by him."[282] - John Locke

---

[280] Locke, Second Treatise of Government. Kindle Location 56 percent of 100

[281] Locke, Second Treatise of Government. Kindle Location 4 percent of 100

[282] Locke, Second Treatise of Government. Kindle Location 5 percent of 100

"...so that laws human must be made according to the general laws of nature, and without contradiction to any positive law of scripture, otherwise they are ill made."[283] – John Locke

On War and Self-Defense:

"He that shall oppose an assault only with a shield to receive the blows, or in any more respectful posture, without a sword in his hand, to abate the confidence and force of the assailant, will quickly be at an end of his resistance, and will find such a defense serve only to draw on himself the worse usage."[284] - John Locke

"...it being reasonable and just, I should have a right to destroy that which threatens me with destruction: for, by the fundamental law of nature, man being to be preserved as much as possible, when all cannot be preserved, the safety of the innocent is to be preferred: and one man may destroy a man who makes war upon him..."[285] - John Locke

"...the law, which was made for my preservation, where it cannot interpose to secure my life from present force, which, if lost, is capable of no reparation, permits me my own defense, and the right of war, a liberty to kill the aggressor..."[286] - John Locke.

Limited Government Power:

"And hence it is, that he who attempts to get another man into his absolute power, does thereby put himself into a state of war with him; it being to be understood as a declaration of a design upon his life: for I have reason to conclude, that he who would get me into his power without my consent, would use me as he pleased when he had got me there..."[287] - John Locke

"For he that thinks absolute power purifies men's blood, and corrects the baseness of human nature, need read but the history of this, or any other age, to be convinced of the contrary."[288] - John Locke

"First, they are to govern by promulgated established laws, not to be varied in particular cases, but to have one rule for rich and poor, for the favourite at court, and for the country man at his plough."[289] - John Locke

"No man in civil society can be exempted from the laws of it..."[290] - John Locke

"Fourthly, the legislative neither must nor can transfer the power of making laws to any body else, or place it any where but where the people have."[291] - John Locke

"This I am sure, whoever, either ruler or subject, by force goes about to invade the rights of either prince or people, and lays the foundation for overturning the constitution and frame of any

[283] Locke, Second Treatise of Government. Kindle Location 56 percent of 100
[284] Locke, Second Treatise of Government. Kindle Location 95 percent of 100
[285] Locke, Second Treatise of Government. Kindle Location 8 percent of 100
[286] Locke, Second Treatise of Government. Kindle Location 9 percent of 100
[287] Locke, Second Treatise of Government. Kindle Location 8 percent of 100
[288] Ibid.
[289] Locke, Second Treatise of Government. Kindle Location 59 percent of 100
[290] Locke, Second Treatise of Government. Kindle Location 39 percent of 100
[291] Locke, Second Treatise of Government. Kindle Location 59 percent of 100

just government, is highly guilty of the greatest crime, I think, a man is capable of..."[292] - John Locke

"They saw, that to live by one man's will, became the cause of all men's misery."[293] - John Locke

"But in governments, where the legislative is in one lasting assembly always being, or in in one man, as in absolute monarchies, there is danger still, that they will think themselves to have a distinct interest from the rest of the community; and so will be apt to increase their own riches and power, by taking what they think fit from the people..."[294] - John Locke

"First, the legislative acts against the trust reposed in them, when they endeavour to invade the property of the subject, and to make themselves, or any part of the community, masters, or arbitrary disposers of the lives, liberties, or fortunes of the people."[295] - John Locke

"Thirdly, the supreme power cannot take from any man any part of his property without his own consent: for the preservation of property being the end of government, and that for which men enter into society, it necessarily supposes and requires, that the people should have property, without which they must be supposed to lose that, by entering into society, which was the end for which they entered into it; too gross an absurdity for any man to own."[296] - John Locke

"Betwixt subject and subject they [others] will grant, there must be measures, laws and judges, for their mutual peace and security: but as for the ruler, he [they think] ought to be absolute, and is above all such circumstances; because he has power to do more hurt and wrong, it is right [they therefore believe] when he does it. To ask how you may be guarded from harm, or injury, on that side where the strongest hand is to do it, is presently the voice of faction and rebellion: as if when men quitting the state of nature entered into society, they agreed that all of them but one, should be under the restraint of laws, but that he should still retain all the liberty of the state of nature, increased with power, and made licentious by impunity. This is to think, that men are so foolish, that they take care to avoid what mischiefs may be done them by pole-cats, or foxes; but are content, nay, think it safety, to be devoured by lions."[297] - John Locke

"Hence it is a mistake to think, that the supreme or legislative power of any common-wealth, can do what it will, and dispose of the estates of the subject arbitrarily, or take any part of them at pleasure."[298] - John Locke

"But because those laws which are constantly to be executed, and whose force is always to continue, may be made in a little time; therefore there is no need, that the legislative should be always in being, not having always business to do."[299] - John Locke

Labor and Ownership of Wealth

---

[292] Locke, Second Treatise of Government. Kindle Location 93 percent of 100
[293] Locke, Second Treatise of Government. Kindle Location 39 percent of 100
[294] Locke, Second Treatise of Government. Kindle Location 58 percent of 100
[295] Locke, Second Treatise of Government. Kindle Location 89 percent of 100
[296] Locke, Second Treatise of Government. Kindle Location 57 percent of 100
[297] Locke, Second Treatise of Government. Kindle Location 38 percent of 100
[298] Locke, Second Treatise of Government. Kindle Location 58 percent of 100
[299] Locke, Second Treatise of Government. Kindle Location 60 percent of 100

"Though the water running in the fountain be every one's, yet who can doubt, but that in the pitcher is his only who drew it out?"[300] - John Locke

"The labour of his body, and the work of his hands, we may say, are properly his."[301] - John Locke

"To which let me add, that he who appropriates land to himself by his labour, does not lessen, but increase the common stock of mankind: for the provisions serving to support of human life, produced by one acre of inclosed and cultivated land, are (to speak much within compass) ten times more than those which are yielded by an acre of land of an equal richness lying waste in common."[302] - John Locke

"Thirdly, the supreme power cannot take from any man any part of his property without his own consent: for the preservation of property being the end of government, and that for which men enter into society, it necessarily supposes and requires, that the people should have property, without which they must be supposed to lose that, by entering into society, which was the end for which they entered into it; too gross an absurdity for any man to own."[303] - John Locke, 1690

Punishment for Transgressions of Natural Law:

"I answer, each transgression may be punished to that degree, and with so much severity, as will suffice to make it an ill bargain to the offender, give him cause to repent, and terrify others from doing the like."[304] - John Locke

On Freedom:

"MEN being, as has been said, by nature, all free, equal, and independent, no one can be put out of this estate, and subjected to the political power of another, without his own consent."[305] - John Locke

"...all peaceful beginnings of government have been laid in the consent of the people."[306] - John Locke

On Citizenship Requiring Legal Affirmation:

"And thus we see, that foreigners, by living all their lives under another government, and enjoying the privileges and protection of it, though they are bound, even in conscience, to submit to its administration, as far forth as any denison; yet do not thereby come to be subjects or members of that commonwealth. Nothing can make any man so, but his actually entering into it by positive engagement, and express promise and compact."[307] - John Locke

[300] Locke, Second Treatise of Government. Kindle Location 13 percent of 100
[301] Locke, Second Treatise of Government. Kindle Location 12 percent of 100
[302] Locke, Second Treatise of Government. Kindle Location 16 percent of 100
[303] Locke, Second Treatise of Government. Kindle Location 57 percent of 100
[304] Locke, Second Treatise of Government. Kindle Location 6 percent of 100
[305] Locke, Second Treatise of Government. Kindle Location 40 percent of 100
[306] Locke, Second Treatise of Government. Kindle Location 47 percent of 100
[307] Locke, Second Treatise of Government. Kindle Location 51 percent of 100

Benjamin Rush, Quotes for Conservatives and Republicans

Benjamin Rush is a founding father whose place in the history books should be more prominent.

A skilled doctor, Rush is considered among the fathers of the field of American psychology.

Prior to the struggle for American independence, he was a member of the Sons of Liberty, an organization whose powerful voice helped lead to the Revolution. He suggested the name for his friend Thomas Paine's pamphlet *Common Sense*,[308] a publication without which the revolutionary cause might never have gotten off the floor.

He represented Pennsylvania in the Continental Congress and signed the Declaration of Independence immediately above the signature of Benjamin Franklin.

During the war, he served as surgeon general to George Washington's army. He worked hard to reform Pennsylvania's Constitution, and would go on after the war to found Dickinson College in Pennsylvania, which still exists today.

Many of his key thoughts and ideas are printed below.

Religion, Morals, Civil Society and Their Effect on Government :

"Let every family in the United States be furnished at the public expense, by the Secretary of this office, with a copy of an American edition of the BIBLE."[309] – Benjamin Rush

"It is now several months, since I promised to give you my reasons for preferring the Bible as a school book, to other compositions."[310] – Benjamin Rush

"I proceed in the next place, to enquire, what mode of education we shall adopt so as to secure to the state all the advantages that are to be derived from the proper instruction of youth; and here I beg leave to remark, that the only foundation for a useful education in a republic is to be laid in Religion. Without this there can be no virtue, and without virtue there can be no liberty, and liberty is the object and life of all republican governments."[311] – Benjamin Rush

"There are errors of an impious nature, which sometimes obtain a currency, from being disguised by innocent names."[312] – Benjamin Rush

---

[308] Runes, The Selected Writings Of Benjamin Rush. Kindle Location 1 percent of 100

[309] Benjamin Rush "A Plan of a Peace-Office for the United States" in The Selected Writings Of Benjamin Rush, ed. Dagobert D. Runes (Amazon Kindle). Kindle Location 6 percent of 100

[310] Benjamin Rush "The Bible as a School Book" in The Selected Writings Of Benjamin Rush, ed. Dagobert D. Runes (Amazon Kindle). Kindle Location 25 percent of 100

[311] Benjamin Rush "Lectures on Animal Life, Lecture III" in The Selected Writings Of Benjamin Rush, ed. Dagobert D. Runes (Amazon Kindle). Kindle Location 38 percent of 100

[312] Benjamin Rush "Of the Mode of Education Proper in a Republic" in The Selected Writings Of Benjamin Rush, ed. Dagobert D. Runes (Amazon Kindle). Kindle Location 19 percent of 100

"Let the following sentence be inscribed in letters of gold over the doors of every State and Court house in the United States. "THE SON OF MAN CAME INTO THE WORLD, NOT TO DESTROY MEN'S LIVES, BUT TO SAVE THEM.""[313] – Benjamin Rush

"I am aware that I dissent from one of those paradoxical opinions with which modern times abound; [which states] that it is improper to fill the minds of youth with religious prejudices of any kind, and that they should be left to choose their own principles [when old enough]...Could we preserve the mind in childhood and youth a perfect blank, this plan of education would have more to recommend it...But I beg leave to ask, why should we pursue a different plan of education with respect to religion, from that which we pursue in teaching the arts and sciences? Do we leave our youth to acquire systems of geography, philosophy, or politics, till they have arrived at an age in which they are capable of judging for themselves? We do not."[314] – Benjamin Rush

"Atheism is the worst of sedatives to the understanding, and passions. It is the abstraction of thought from the most sublime, and of love, from the most perfect of all possible objects...The necessary and immutable connection between the texture of the human mind, and the worship of an object of some kind, has lately been demonstrated by the atheists of Europe, who after rejecting the true God, have instituted the worship of nature, of fortune, and of human reason; and in some instances, with ceremonies of the most expensive and splendid kind."[315] – Benjamin Rush

"It is foreign to my purpose to hint at the arguments which establish the truth of the Christian revelation. My only business is to declare, that all its doctrines and precepts are calculated to promote the happiness of society, and the safety and well being of civil government. A Christian cannot fail of being a republican."[316] – Benjamin Rush

"A Christian cannot fail of being useful to the republic, for his religion teacheth him, that no man "liveth to himself."[317] – Benjamin Rush

"Let the youth of our country be carefully instructed in reading, writing, arithmetic, and in the doctrines of a religion of some kind: the Christian religion should be preferred to all others; for it belongs to this religion exclusively to teach us not only to cultivate peace with men, but to forgive, nay more – to love our very enemies."[318] – Benjamin Rush

"The plan for the free schools is taken chiefly from the plans which have long been used with success in Scotland and in the eastern states of America, where the influence of learning, in

---

[313] Benjamin Rush "A Plan of a Peace-Office for the United States" in The Selected Writings Of Benjamin Rush, ed. Dagobert D. Runes (Amazon Kindle). Kindle Location 6 percent of 100.

[314] Benjamin Rush "Of the Mode of Education Proper in a Republic" in The Selected Writings Of Benjamin Rush, ed. Dagobert D. Runes (Amazon Kindle). Kindle Location 20 percent of 100

[315] Benjamin Rush "Lectures on Animal Life, Lecture III" in The Selected Writings Of Benjamin Rush, ed. Dagobert D. Runes (Amazon Kindle). Kindle Location 36 percent of 100

[316] Benjamin Rush "Of the Mode of Education Proper in a Republic" in The Selected Writings Of Benjamin Rush, ed. Dagobert D. Runes (Amazon Kindle). Kindle Location 19 percent of 100

[317] Benjamin Rush "Of the Mode of Education Proper in a Republic" in The Selected Writings Of Benjamin Rush, ed. Dagobert D. Runes (Amazon Kindle). Kindle Location 20 percent of 100

[318] Benjamin Rush "A Plan of a Peace-Office for the United States" in The Selected Writings Of Benjamin Rush, ed. Dagobert D. Runes (Amazon Kindle). Kindle Location 6 percent of 100

promoting religion, morals, manners and good government, has never been exceeded in any country."[319] – Benjamin Rush

"Let every man exert himself in promoting virtue and knowledge in our country, and we shall soon become good republicans."[320] – Benjamin Rush

"The law was not only neglected, but lost during the general profligacy of manners which accompanied the long and wicked reign of Manassah. But the discovery of it, in the rubbish of the temple, by Josiah, and its subsequent general use, were followed by a return of national virtue and prosperity."[321] – Benjamin Rush

"...Christianity is the only true and perfect religion, and...in proportion as mankind adopt its principles, and obey its precepts, they will be wise, and happy."[322] – Benjamin Rush

"We err not only in human affairs, but in religion likewise, *only* because "we do not know the scriptures."[323] – Benjamin Rush

"The memory is the first faculty which opens in the minds of children. Of how much consequence, then, must it be, to impress it with the great truths of Christianity, before it is preoccupied with less interesting subjects!"[324] – Benjamin Rush

"We hear much of the persons educated in free schools in England, turning out well in the various walks of life. I have enquired into the cause of it, and have satisfied myself, that it is wholly to be ascribed to the general use of the Bible in those schools, for it seems the children of poor people are of too little consequence to be guarded from the supposed evils of reading the scriptures in early life, or in an unconsecrated school house."[325] – Benjamin Rush

"The moral faculty exercises itself upon the actions of others...while conscience confines its operations only to its own actions. These two capacities of the mind...sometimes exist in different degrees in the same person. Hence we often find conscience in its full vigour, with a diminished tone, or total absence of the moral faculty."[326] – Benjamin Rush

"The boasted morality of the deists is, I believe, in most cases, the offspring of habits, produced originally by the principles and precepts of Christianity."[327] – Benjamin Rush

---

[319] Benjamin Rush "Education Agreeable to a Republican Form of Government" in The Selected Writings Of Benjamin Rush, ed. Dagobert D. Runes (Amazon Kindle). Kindle Location 22 percent of 100

[320] Benjamin Rush "On the Defects of the Confederation" in The Selected Writings Of Benjamin Rush, ed. Dagobert D. Runes (Amazon Kindle). Kindle Location 8 percent of 100

[321] Benjamin Rush "The Bible as a School Book" in The Selected Writings Of Benjamin Rush, ed. Dagobert D. Runes (Amazon Kindle). Kindle Location 26 percent of 100

[322] Benjamin Rush "The Bible as a School Book" in The Selected Writings Of Benjamin Rush, ed. Dagobert D. Runes (Amazon Kindle). Kindle Location 25 percent of 100

[323] Benjamin Rush "The Bible as a School Book" in The Selected Writings Of Benjamin Rush, ed. Dagobert D. Runes (Amazon Kindle). Kindle Location 26 percent of 100

[324] Benjamin Rush "The Bible as a School Book" in The Selected Writings Of Benjamin Rush, ed. Dagobert D. Runes (Amazon Kindle). Kindle Location 25 percent of 100

[325] Benjamin Rush "The Bible as a School Book" in The Selected Writings Of Benjamin Rush, ed. Dagobert D. Runes (Amazon Kindle). Kindle Location 28 percent of 100

[326] Benjamin Rush "The Influence of Physical Causes Upon the Moral Faculty" in The Selected Writings Of Benjamin Rush, ed. Dagobert D. Runes (Amazon Kindle). Kindle Location 39 percent of 100

"But the religion I mean to recommend in this place, is that of the New Testament."[328] – Benjamin Rush

"If we descend from nations to sects, we shall find them wise and prosperous in proportion as they become early acquainted with the scriptures."[329] – Benjamin Rush

"Never publish an article in your paper, that you would not wish your wife or daughter (if you have any) should read or understand."[330] – Benjamin Rush

"I grant this mode of secluding boys from the intercourse of private families, has a tendency to make them scholars, but our business is to make them men, citizens and Christians."[331] – Benjamin Rush

"...[T]he bible contains more knowledge necessary to man in his present state, than any other book in the world."[332] – Benjamin Rush

"...[T]he morality of the Deists, which has been so much admired and praised, is, I believe, in most cases, the effect of habits, produced by early instruction in the principles of Christianity."[333] – Benjamin Rush

"There is a native love of truth in the human mind." [334] – Benjamin Rush

"I wish to be excused for repeating here, that if the Bible did not convey a single direction for the attainment of future happiness, it should be read in our schools in preference to all other books, from, its containing the greatest portion of that kind of knowledge which is calculated to produce private and public temporal happiness."[335] – Benjamin Rush

"The best criterion of the truth of a philosophical opinion, is its tendency to produce exalted ideas, of the Divine Being, and humble views of ourselves."[336] – Benjamin Rush

"O! nature! – Or to speak more properly, - O! Thou God of Nature!"[337] – Benjamin Rush

---

[327] Benjamin Rush "The Influence of Physical Causes Upon the Moral Faculty" in The Selected Writings Of Benjamin Rush, ed. Dagobert D. Runes (Amazon Kindle). Kindle Location 43 percent of 100

[328] Benjamin Rush "Of the Mode of Education Proper in a Republic" in The Selected Writings Of Benjamin Rush, ed. Dagobert D. Runes (Amazon Kindle). Kindle Location 19 percent of 100

[329] Ibid.

[330] Benjamin Rush "Directions for Conducting a Newspaper" in The Selected Writings Of Benjamin Rush, ed. Dagobert D. Runes (Amazon Kindle). Kindle Location 85 percent of 100

[331] Benjamin Rush "Of the Mode of Education Proper in a Republic" in The Selected Writings Of Benjamin Rush, ed. Dagobert D. Runes (Amazon Kindle). Kindle Location 20 percent of 100

[332] Benjamin Rush "The Bible as a School Book" in The Selected Writings Of Benjamin Rush, ed. Dagobert D. Runes (Amazon Kindle). Kindle Location 25 percent of 100

[333] Benjamin Rush "The Bible as a School Book" in The Selected Writings Of Benjamin Rush, ed. Dagobert D. Runes (Amazon Kindle). Kindle Location 26 percent of 100

[334] Ibid.

[335] Ibid.

[336] Benjamin Rush "Lectures on Animal Life, Lecture III" in The Selected Writings Of Benjamin Rush, ed. Dagobert D. Runes (Amazon Kindle). Kindle Location 38 percent of 100

[337] Benjamin Rush "The Influence of Physical Causes Upon the Moral Faculty" in The Selected Writings Of Benjamin

"Religion and morals, government and liberty, nay, even reason and the senses, so happily paired by the Creator of the world, in the order in which they have been mentioned, have each been disunited by the caprice and folly of man."[338] - Benjamin Rush

"The many artful attacks which have been made upon Christianity by the Deistical writers in England instead of lessening its credibility have tended rather to establish it by drawing forth some of the most learned publications in its defense which have ever appeared upon any subjects whatever."[339] – Benjamin Rush

"An undue confidence in medicine, to the exclusion of a Divine and Superintending Power over the health and lives of men, is another vice among physicians."[340] – Benjamin Rush

"...[T]he profession of medicine, favours the practice of all the religious, moral and social duties."[341] – Benjamin Rush

"Whenever you are called, therefore, to visit a poor patient, imagine you hear the voice of the good Samaritan sounding in your ears, "Take care of him, and I will repay thee."[342] – Benjamin Rush

"Dr. Heberdeen's liberality to the poor was so great, that he was once told by a friend, that he would exhaust his fortune. "No," said he, "after all my charities, I am afraid I shall die *shamefully* rich."[343] – Benjamin Rush

"Thus we see poverty and misery, crimes and infamy, diseases and death, are all the natural and usual consequences of the intemperate use of ardent spirits."[344] – Benjamin Rush

"A belief in God's providence and a constant reliance upon his power and goodness, impart a composure and firmness to the mind which render it incapable of being moved by all the real, or imaginary evils of life."[345] – Benjamin Rush

On Limited Government:

Rush, ed. Dagobert D. Runes (Amazon Kindle). Kindle Location 44 percent of 100

[338] Benjamin Rush "Observations and Reasoning in Medicine, A Lecture" in The Selected Writings Of Benjamin Rush, ed. Dagobert D. Runes (Amazon Kindle). Kindle Location 53 percent of 100

[339] Benjamin Rush "From a Diary Traveling Through France" in The Selected Writings Of Benjamin Rush, ed. Dagobert D. Runes (Amazon Kindle). Kindle Location 82 percent of 100

[340] Benjamin Rush "The Vices and Virtues of Physicians, A Lecture" in The Selected Writings Of Benjamin Rush, ed. Dagobert D. Runes (Amazon Kindle). Kindle Location 64 percent of 100

[341] Benjamin Rush "The Vices and Virtues of Physicians, A Lecture" in The Selected Writings Of Benjamin Rush, ed. Dagobert D. Runes (Amazon Kindle). Kindle Location 67 percent of 100

[342] Benjamin Rush "Duties of a Physician, A Closing Lecture to Medical Students" in The Selected Writings Of Benjamin Rush, ed. Dagobert D. Runes (Amazon Kindle). Kindle Location 69 percent of 100

[343] Benjamin Rush "The Vices and Virtues of Physicians, A Lecture" in The Selected Writings Of Benjamin Rush, ed. Dagobert D. Runes (Amazon Kindle). Kindle Location 66 percent of 100

[344] Benjamin Rush "The Effects of Ardent Spirits Upon Man" in The Selected Writings Of Benjamin Rush, ed. Dagobert D. Runes (Amazon Kindle). Kindle Location 73 percent of 100

[345] Benjamin Rush "On the Different Species of Phobia" in The Selected Writings Of Benjamin Rush, ed. Dagobert D. Runes (Amazon Kindle). Kindle Location 49 percent of 100

"The American War is over: but this is far from being the case with the American Revolution."[346] – Benjamin Rush

"The minority would give laws to a majority. A solecism [mistake] in government!"[347] – Benjamin Rush

"Let us beware of being imposed upon by the popular cry of the *necessity of the times.*"[348] – Benjamin Rush

"Neither the House of Representatives, the Senate, or the President, can perform a single legislative act by themselves."[349] – Benjamin Rush

"How long mankind may continue to prefer substituted pursuits and pleasures...is uncertain; but the time we are assured will come, when the understanding shall be elevated from its present inferior objects, and the luxated passions be reduced to their original order. – This change in the mind of man, I believe, will be effected only by the influence of the Christian religion, after all the efforts of human reason to produce it, by means of civilization, philosophy, liberty, and government, have been exhausted to no purpose."[350] – Benjamin Rush

"It would have been a truth, if Mr. Locke had not said it, that where there is no law, there can be no liberty; and nothing deserves the name of law but that which is certain, and universal in its operation, upon all the members of the community."[351] – Benjamin Rush

"When natural liberty is given up for laws which enslave instead of protecting us, we are immense losers by the exchange."[352] – Benjamin Rush

"A despotic government is the most simple government in the world, but instead of affording security to property, liberty or life, it obliges us to hold them all on the simple will of a capricious sovereign."[353] – Benjamin Rush

"The Supreme Being alone is qualified to possess supreme power over his creatures. It requires the wisdom and goodness of a Deity to control, and direct it properly."[354] – Benjamin Rush

---

[346] Benjamin Rush "On the Defects of the Confederation" in The Selected Writings Of Benjamin Rush, ed. Dagobert D. Runes (Amazon Kindle). Kindle Location 7 percent of 100

[347] Benjamin Rush "Observations on the Government of Pennsylvania" in The Selected Writings Of Benjamin Rush, ed. Dagobert D. Runes (Amazon Kindle). Kindle Location 17 percent of 100

[348] Benjamin Rush "Observations on the Government of Pennsylvania" in The Selected Writings Of Benjamin Rush, ed. Dagobert D. Runes (Amazon Kindle). Kindle Location 18 percent of 100

[349] Benjamin Rush "Letter from Dr. Rush to Dr. Ramsay" in The Selected Writings Of Benjamin Rush, ed. Dagobert D. Runes (Amazon Kindle). Kindle Location 8 percent of 100

[350] Benjamin Rush "Lectures on Animal Life, Lecture III" in The Selected Writings Of Benjamin Rush, ed. Dagobert D. Runes (Amazon Kindle). Kindle Location 37 percent of 100

[351] Benjamin Rush "Letter from Dr. Rush to Dr. Ramsay" in The Selected Writings Of Benjamin Rush, ed. Dagobert D. Runes (Amazon Kindle). Kindle Location 8 percent of 100

[352] Benjamin Rush "Medicine Among the Indians of North America, A Discussion" in The Selected Writings Of Benjamin Rush, ed. Dagobert D. Runes (Amazon Kindle). Kindle Location 60 percent of 100

[353] Benjamin Rush "Observations on the Government of Pennsylvania" in The Selected Writings Of Benjamin Rush, ed. Dagobert D. Runes (Amazon Kindle). Kindle Location 14 percent of 100

[354] Benjamin Rush "Observations on the Government of Pennsylvania" in The Selected Writings Of Benjamin Rush,

"Thus the humble but true origin of power in the people, is often forgotten in the splendor and pride of governments."[355] – Benjamin Rush

"I cannot help commending the zeal that appears in my countrymen against the power of a King or a House of Lords. I concur with them in all their prejudices against hereditary titles, honour and power."[356] – Benjamin Rush

"When a declaration of independence last summer appeared to be the only measure that could save America, the Tories and moderate men acknowledged the justice of our separation from Great Britain, but said, "This is not the time."[357] – Benjamin Rush

"Let LEGISLATORS, reflect upon the trust reposed in them. Let their laws be made after the spirit of religion – liberty – and our most excellent English Constitution."[358] – Benjamin Rush

"There was a time when the Parliaments of France were as free and independent as our own, but what will not bribery and corruption accomplish."[359] – Benjamin Rush

"Farewell to Liberty, when the sacred bulwarks of a Constitution can be invaded by a legislature!"[360]- Benjamin Rush

"Absolute power should never be trusted to man. It has perverted the wisest heads, and corrupted the best hearts in the world."[361] – Benjamin Rush

"He must love family honor, but he must be taught that neither the rank nor antiquity of his ancestors, can command respect, without personal merit."[362] – Benjamin Rush

On Labor, Ownership of Wealth and Economics:

"Had God abandoned [man] to idleness, he would have entailed tenfold misery upon him."[363] – Benjamin Rush

---

ed. Dagobert D. Runes (Amazon Kindle). Kindle Location 13 percent of 100

[355] Benjamin Rush "Lectures on Animal Life, Lecture III" in The Selected Writings Of Benjamin Rush, ed. Dagobert D. Runes (Amazon Kindle). Kindle Location 37 percent of 100

[356] Benjamin Rush "Observations on the Government of Pennsylvania" in The Selected Writings Of Benjamin Rush, ed. Dagobert D. Runes (Amazon Kindle). Kindle Location 14 percent of 100

[357] Benjamin Rush "Observations on the Government of Pennsylvania" in The Selected Writings Of Benjamin Rush, ed. Dagobert D. Runes (Amazon Kindle). Kindle Location 18 percent of 100

[358] Benjamin Rush "On Slave-Keeping" in The Selected Writings Of Benjamin Rush, ed. Dagobert D. Runes (Amazon Kindle). Kindle Location 3 percent of 100

[359] Benjamin Rush "From a Diary Traveling Through France" in The Selected Writings Of Benjamin Rush, ed. Dagobert D. Runes (Amazon Kindle). Kindle Location 81 percent of 100

[360] Benjamin Rush "Observations on the Government of Pennsylvania" in The Selected Writings Of Benjamin Rush, ed. Dagobert D. Runes (Amazon Kindle). Kindle Location 13 percent of 100

[361] Ibid.

[362] Benjamin Rush "Of the Mode of Education Proper in a Republic" in The Selected Writings Of Benjamin Rush, ed. Dagobert D. Runes (Amazon Kindle). Kindle Location 20 percent of 100

[363] Benjamin Rush "Sermon on Exercise" in The Selected Writings Of Benjamin Rush, ed. Dagobert D. Runes (Amazon Kindle). Kindle Location 77 percent of 100

"If we consider the commerce of our metropolis only as the avenue of the wealth of the state, the study of it merits a place in a young man's education; but, I consider commerce in a much higher light when I recommend the study of it in republican seminaries. I view it as the best security against the influence of hereditary monopolies of land, and, therefore, the surest protection against aristocracy. I consider its effects as next to those of religion in humanizing mankind, and lastly, I view it as the means of uniting the different nations of the world together by the ties of mutual wants and obligations."[364] – Benjamin Rush

"Liberty and property form the basis of abundance, and good agriculture: I never observed it to flourish where those rights of mankind were not firmly established."[365] – Benjamin Rush

"Labor of all kinds favors and facilitates the practice of virtue."[366] – Benjamin Rush

"Here the feeling heart, the tearful eye, and the charitable hand, may always be connected together, and the flame of sympathy, instead of being extinguished in taxes, or expiring in a solitary blaze by a single contribution, may be kept alive by constant exercise."[367] – Benjamin Rush

"Let the advancement of agriculture – manufactures – and commerce, be the principal objects of your [news]paper."[368] – Benjamin Rush

On National Defense:

"Let masters be employed likewise to teach gunnery – fortification – and every thing connected with defensive and offensive war."[369] – Benjamin Rush

On Patriotism:

"Next to the duty which young men owe to their Creator, I wish to see a regard to their country, inculcated upon them."[370] – Benjamin Rush

"Our country includes family, friends and property, and should be preferred to them all."[371] – Benjamin Rush

"I do not wish to see our youth educated with a single prejudice against any nation or country; but we impose a task upon human nature, repugnant alike to reason, revelation and the

---

[364] Benjamin Rush "Of the Mode of Education Proper in a Republic" in The Selected Writings Of Benjamin Rush, ed. Dagobert D. Runes (Amazon Kindle). Kindle Location 21 percent of 100

[365] Benjamin Rush "On Slave-Keeping" in The Selected Writings Of Benjamin Rush, ed. Dagobert D. Runes (Amazon Kindle). Kindle Location 2 percent of 100

[366] Benjamin Rush "The Influence of Physical Causes Upon the Moral Faculty" in The Selected Writings Of Benjamin Rush, ed. Dagobert D. Runes (Amazon Kindle). Kindle Location 42 percent of 100

[367] Benjamin Rush "The Influence of Physical Causes Upon the Moral Faculty" in The Selected Writings Of Benjamin Rush, ed. Dagobert D. Runes (Amazon Kindle). Kindle Location 44 percent of 100

[368] Benjamin Rush "Directions for Conducting a Newspaper" in The Selected Writings Of Benjamin Rush, ed. Dagobert D. Runes (Amazon Kindle). Kindle Location 85 percent of 100

[369] Benjamin Rush "On the Defects of the Confederation" in The Selected Writings Of Benjamin Rush, ed. Dagobert D. Runes (Amazon Kindle). Kindle Location 7 percent of 100

[370] Benjamin Rush "Of the Mode of Education Proper in a Republic" in The Selected Writings Of Benjamin Rush, ed. Dagobert D. Runes (Amazon Kindle). Kindle Location 20 percent of 100

[371] Ibid.

ordinary dimensions of the human heart, when require him to embrace, with equal affection, the whole family of mankind."[372] – Benjamin Rush

"While we inculcate these republican duties upon our pupil, we must not neglect, at the same time, to inspire him with republican principles. He must be taught that there can be no durable liberty but in a republic..."[373] – Benjamin Rush

America the Exceptional:

"The liberty of the whole world is the price for which we fight. Human nature looks to us to avenge the mighty ills she has suffered from the tyrants of the old world."[374] – Benjamin Rush

"Remember the eyes of all Europe are fixed upon you, to preserve an asylum for freedom in this country, after the last pillars of it are fallen in every other quarter of the globe."[375] – Benjamin Rush

"It was generally believed by the friends of the Revolution, that the very existence of *freedom* upon our globe, was involved in the issue of the contest in favor of the United States."[376] – Benjamin Rush

"It is impossible to tell from history, what will be the effects of agriculture, industry, temperance, and commerce, urged on by the competition of colonies, united in the same general pursuits, in a country, which for extent, variety of soil, climate and number of navigable rivers, has never been equaled in any quarter of the globe."[377] – Benjamin Rush

On Education:

"To oblige a sprightly boy to sit *seven* hours in a day, with his little arms pinioned to his sides, and his neck unnaturally bent towards his book; and for *no crime!* – what cruelty and folly are manifested, by such an absurd mode of instruction or governing young people!"[378] – Benjamin Rush

"If these punishments fail of reclaiming a bad boy, he should be dismissed from school, to prevent his corrupting his schoolmates. It is the business of parents, and not of school-masters, to use the last means for eradicating idleness and vice from their children."[379] – Benjamin Rush

---

[372] Ibid.

[373] Ibid.

[374] Benjamin Rush "Observations on the Government of Pennsylvania" in The Selected Writings Of Benjamin Rush, ed. Dagobert D. Runes (Amazon Kindle). Kindle Location 18 percent of 100

[375] Benjamin Rush "On Slave-Keeping" in The Selected Writings Of Benjamin Rush, ed. Dagobert D. Runes (Amazon Kindle). Kindle Location 3 percent of 100

[376] Benjamin Rush "Influence of the American Revolution" in The Selected Writings Of Benjamin Rush, ed. Dagobert D. Runes (Amazon Kindle). Kindle Location 70 percent of 100

[377] Benjamin Rush "Medicine Among the Indians of North America, A Discussion" in The Selected Writings Of Benjamin Rush, ed. Dagobert D. Runes (Amazon Kindle). Kindle Location 61 percent of 100

[378] Benjamin Rush "The Amusements and Punishments Which are Proper for Schools" in The Selected Writings Of Benjamin Rush, ed. Dagobert D. Runes (Amazon Kindle). Kindle Location 24 percent of 100

[379] Benjamin Rush "The Amusements and Punishments Which are Proper for Schools" in The Selected Writings Of Benjamin Rush, ed. Dagobert D. Runes (Amazon Kindle). Kindle Location 25 percent of 100

"The sciences have been compared to a circle of which religion composes a part. To understand any one of them perfectly it is necessary to have some knowledge of them all."[380] – Benjamin Rush

"Under the first head I shall begin by lamenting, that men whose educations necessarily open to them the wisdom and goodness of the Creator, and whose duties lead them constantly to behold his power over human life, and all its comforts, should be so very prone to forget him."[381] – Benjamin Rush

On Slavery:

"So MUCH hath been said upon the subject of Slave-keeping, that an apology may be required for this paper. The only one I shall offer is, that the evil still continues."[382] – Benjamin Rush

"Let such, therefore, who vindicate the traffic of buying and selling souls, seek some modern system of religion to support it, and not presume to sanctify their crimes by attempting to reconcile it to the sublime and perfect Religion of the Great Author of Christianity."[383] – Benjamin Rush

"Let such of our countrymen as engage in the slave trade, be shunned as the greatest enemies to our country, and, let the vessels which bring the slaves to us, be avoided as if they bore in them the seeds of that forbidden fruit, whose baneful taste destroyed both the natural and moral world."[384] – Benjamin Rush

"Such is the will of the great Author of our Nature, who has created man free, and assigned to him the earth, that he might cultivate his possession with the sweat of his brow; but still should enjoy his Liberty."[385] – Benjamin Rush

---

[380] Benjamin Rush "The Bible as a School Book" in The Selected Writings Of Benjamin Rush, ed. Dagobert D. Runes (Amazon Kindle). Kindle Location 27 percent of 100

[381] Benjamin Rush "The Vices and Virtues of Physicians, A Lecture" in The Selected Writings Of Benjamin Rush, ed. Dagobert D. Runes (Amazon Kindle). Kindle Location 64 percent of 100

[382] Benjamin Rush "On Slave-Keeping" in The Selected Writings Of Benjamin Rush, ed. Dagobert D. Runes (Amazon Kindle). Kindle Location 1 percent of 100

[383] Benjamin Rush "On Slave-Keeping" in The Selected Writings Of Benjamin Rush, ed. Dagobert D. Runes (Amazon Kindle). Kindle Location 2 percent of 100

[384] Benjamin Rush "On Slave-Keeping" in The Selected Writings Of Benjamin Rush, ed. Dagobert D. Runes (Amazon Kindle). Kindle Location 3 percent of 100

[385] Benjamin Rush "On Slave-Keeping" in The Selected Writings Of Benjamin Rush, ed. Dagobert D. Runes (Amazon Kindle). Kindle Location 2 percent of 100

Thomas Jefferson, Quotes for Conservatives and Republicans:

Thomas Jefferson is perhaps best known for having written the Declaration of Independence (aided by a committee that included Benjamin Franklin and John Adams, whose ideas are also included in these pages). His words – simple but beautiful prose that lays out the basic rights of man and the fundamental theory of democratic government – will forever resound among those who love freedom.

Although only thirty-three when he wrote the declaration, Jefferson's later career was hardly less illustrious. Just three years later, he was elected governor of Virginia. Following the Revolutionary War, he served again in the Continental Congress, and also served as the American ambassador to France during the years leading up to the French Revolution.

Upon returning home, he took up the post of Secretary of State of the United States, the first man ever to hold that job. He then became America's second vice-president, helping while in that role to draft procedural rules for the newly formed United States Senate.

In 1801, Jefferson became the third president of the United States. During his presidency, he helped double the size of the United States by agreeing with France to the terms of the Louisiana Purchase. To make sure the new territory was thoroughly mapped and explored, he then commissioned the now famous Lewis and Clark expedition.

Although often cited as a proponent of strict separation between church and state, Jefferson's views on the subject were born in significant part from frustration over a law in his native Virginia that used tax dollars to support a specific denomination for the purpose of establishing it as the official religion of Virginia. This was significantly different from the type of regulation that merely allows one of America's states to interact with a religious organization for the charitable benefit of the poor, or promote general religious belief by requesting a day of prayer in response to a tragedy – both of which concepts have been implemented by modern conservatives.

Jefferson's ideas on these and other matters differ markedly from how his beliefs are commonly presented to students and the modern public, as demonstrated by his words below.

On Limited Government:

"The inspectors of internal revenue who were found to obstruct the accountability of the institution have been discontinued."[386] – Thomas Jefferson

"Were not this great country already divided into states, that division must be made, that each might do for itself what concerns itself directly, and what it can so much better do than a distant authority. Every state again is divided into counties, each to take care of what lies within its local bounds; each county again into townships or wards, to manage minuter details; and every ward into farms, to be governed each by its individual proprietor. Were we directed from Washington when to sow, and when to reap, we should soon want bread."[387] – Thomas Jefferson

---

[386] Thomas Jefferson "State of the Union Address, Dec. 8, 1801" in State of the Union Address, Thomas Jefferson, A Public Domain Book, (Amazon Kindle), Kindle Location 5 percent of 100.

"The true theory of our constitution is surely the wisest and best, that the States are independent as to every thing within themselves, and united as to every thing respecting foreign nations. Let the General Government be reduced to foreign concerns only..."[388] – Thomas Jefferson

"I suppose an amendment to the Constitution, by consent of the States, necessary, because the objects now recommended are not among those enumerated in the Constitution, and to which it permits the public moneys to be applied."[389] – Thomas Jefferson

"To make us one nation as to foreign concerns, and keep us distinct in domestic ones, gives the outline of the proper division of powers between the general and particular [state] governments."[390] – Thomas Jefferson

"I own, I am not a friend to a very energetic government. It is always oppressive."[391] – Thomas Jefferson
"The limited powers of the federal government, and jealousy of the subordinate [state] governments, afford a security which exists in no other instance." – Thomas Jefferson[392]

"We have thought, hitherto, that the roads of a State could not be so well administered even by the State legislature as by the magistracy of the county, on the spot."[393] – Thomas Jefferson

"There is a remarkable difference between the characters of the inconveniences which attend a declaration of rights, and those which attend the want of it. The inconveniences of the declaration are, that it may cramp government in its useful exertions. But the evil of this is short-lived, moderate, and reparable. The inconveniences of the want of a declaration are permanent, afflicting, and irreparable. They are in constant progression from bad to worse."[394] – Thomas Jefferson

---

[387] Thomas Jefferson "Memoir" in Memoir, Correspondence, And Miscellanies, From The Papers Of Thomas Jefferson, Volume I, ed. Thomas Jefferson Randolph (Amazon Kindle), Kindle Location 17 percent of 100.
[388] Thomas Jefferson "Letter to Gideon Granger, 1800" in Memoir, Correspondence, And Miscellanies, From The Papers Of Thomas Jefferson, Volume III, ed. Thomas Jefferson Randolph (Amazon Kindle), Kindle Location 85 percent of 100.
[389] Thomas Jefferson "State of the Union Address, Dec. 2, 1806" in State of the Union Address, Thomas Jefferson, A Public Domain Book, (Amazon Kindle), Kindle Location 72 percent of 100.
[390] Thomas Jefferson "Letter to James Madison, 1786" in Memoir, Correspondence, And Miscellanies, From The Papers Of Thomas Jefferson, Volume II, ed. Thomas Jefferson Randolph (Amazon Kindle), Kindle Location 14 percent of 100.
[391] Thomas Jefferson "Letter to James Madison, 1787" in Memoir, Correspondence, And Miscellanies, From The Papers Of Thomas Jefferson, Volume II, ed. Thomas Jefferson Randolph (Amazon Kindle), Kindle Location 56 percent of 100.
[392] Thomas Jefferson "Letter to James Madison, 1789" in Memoir, Correspondence, And Miscellanies, From The Papers Of Thomas Jefferson, Volume II, ed. Thomas Jefferson Randolph (Amazon Kindle), Kindle Location 89 percent of 100.
[393] Thomas Jefferson "Letter to James Madison, 1796" in Memoir, Correspondence, And Miscellanies, From The Papers Of Thomas Jefferson, Volume III, ed. Thomas Jefferson Randolph (Amazon Kindle), Kindle Location 63 percent of 100.
[394] Thomas Jefferson "Letter to James Madison, 1789" in Memoir, Correspondence, And Miscellanies, From The Papers Of Thomas Jefferson, Volume II, ed. Thomas Jefferson Randolph (Amazon Kindle), Kindle Location 89 percent of 100.

"I have no fear, but that the result of our experiment will be, that men may be trusted to govern themselves without a master."[395] – Thomas Jefferson

" Among those who are dependent on Executive discretion I have begun the reduction of what was deemed unnecessary. The expenses of diplomatic agency have been considerably diminished."[396] – Thomas Jefferson

"...I indulge the pleasing persuasion that the great body of our citizens will cordially concur in honest and disinterested efforts which have for their object to preserve the General and State Governments in their constitutional form and equilibrium...and to reduce expenses to what is necessary for the useful purposes of Government."[397] – Thomas Jefferson

"The people are the only censors of their governors; and even their errors will tend to keep these to the true principles of their institution. To punish these errors too severely, would be to suppress the only safeguard of the public liberty."[398] – Thomas Jefferson

"And what country can preserve its liberties, if its rulers are not warned from time to time, that this people preserve the spirit of resistance."[399] – Thomas Jefferson

"When the representative body have lost the confidence of their constituents, when they have notoriously made sale of their most valuable rights, when they have assumed to themselves powers which the people never put into their hands, then, indeed, their continuing in office becomes dangerous to the state, and calls for an exercise of the power of dissolution."[400] – Thomas Jefferson

"But can his Majesty thus put down all law under his feet? Can he erect a power superior to that which erected himself? He has done it indeed by force; but let him remember that force cannot give right."[401] – Thomas Jefferson

---

[395] Thomas Jefferson "Letter to David Hartley, 1787" in Memoir, Correspondence, And Miscellanies, From The Papers Of Thomas Jefferson, Volume II, ed. Thomas Jefferson Randolph (Amazon Kindle), Kindle Location 36 percent of 100.

[396] Thomas Jefferson "State of the Union Address, Dec. 8, 1801" in State of the Union Address, Thomas Jefferson, A Public Domain Book, (Amazon Kindle), Kindle Location 5 percent of 100..

[397] Thomas Jefferson "State of the Union Address, Dec. 8, 1801" in State of the Union Address, Thomas Jefferson, A Public Domain Book, (Amazon Kindle), Kindle Location 14 percent of 100.

[398] Thomas Jefferson "Letter to Colonel Edward Carrington, 1787" in Memoir, Correspondence, And Miscellanies, From The Papers Of Thomas Jefferson, Volume II, ed. Thomas Jefferson Randolph (Amazon Kindle), Kindle Location 18 percent of 100.

[399] Thomas Jefferson "Letter to Colonel Smith, 1787" in Memoir, Correspondence, And Miscellanies, From The Papers Of Thomas Jefferson, Volume II, ed. Thomas Jefferson Randolph (Amazon Kindle), Kindle Location 55 percent of 100.

[400] Thomas Jefferson "Appendix to the Memoir, Instructions to the first Delegation" in Memoir, Correspondence, And Miscellanies, From The Papers Of Thomas Jefferson, Volume I, ed. Thomas Jefferson Randolph (Amazon Kindle), Kindle Location 27 percent of 100.

[401] Thomas Jefferson "Appendix to the Memoir, Instructions to the first Delegation" in Memoir, Correspondence, And Miscellanies, From The Papers Of Thomas Jefferson, Volume I, ed. Thomas Jefferson Randolph (Amazon Kindle), Kindle Location 28 percent of 100.

"...[T]hat to secure these rights, governments are instituted among men, deriving their just powers from the consent of the governed..."[402] – Thomas Jefferson

"I apprehend too, that the total abandonment of the principle of rotation in the offices of President and Senator, will end in abuse."[403] – Thomas Jefferson

"I am for a government rigorously frugal and simple, applying all the possible savings of the public revenue to the discharge of the national debt: and not for a multiplication of officers and salaries merely to make partisans, and for increasing, by every device, the public debt, on the principle of its being a public blessing."[404] – Thomas Jefferson

"...[S]hould a President consent to be a candidate for a third election, I trust he would be rejected, on this demonstration of ambitious views."[405] – Thomas Jefferson

"These rogues set out with stealing the peoples' good opinion, and then steal from them the right of withdrawing it, by contriving laws and associations against the power of the people themselves."[406] – Thomas Jefferson

"...[W]ere it left to me to decide, whether we should have a government without newspapers, or newspapers without a government, I should not hesitate a moment to prefer the latter."[407] – Thomas Jefferson

"Cherish, therefore, the spirit of our people, and keep alive their attention...If once they become inattentive to the public affairs, you, and I, and Congress, and Assemblies, Judges and Governors, shall all become wolves."[408] – Thomas Jefferson

"The second feature I dislike, and strongly dislike, is the abandonment, in every instance, of the principle of rotation in office, and most particularly in the case of the President. Reason and experience tell us, that the first magistrate will always be re-elected if he may be re-elected. He is then an officer for life."[409] – Thomas Jefferson

---

[402] Thomas Jefferson "A Declaration by the Representatives of the United States of America, in General Congress Assembled" in Memoir, Correspondence, And Miscellanies, From The Papers Of Thomas Jefferson, Volume I, ed. Thomas Jefferson Randolph (Amazon Kindle), Kindle Location 6 percent of 100.

[403] Thomas Jefferson "Letter to E. Rutledge, 1788" in Memoir, Correspondence, And Miscellanies, From The Papers Of Thomas Jefferson, Volume II, ed. Thomas Jefferson Randolph (Amazon Kindle), Kindle Location 69 percent of 100.

[404] Thomas Jefferson "Letter to Elbridge Gerry, 1799" in Memoir, Correspondence, And Miscellanies, From The Papers Of Thomas Jefferson, Volume III, ed. Thomas Jefferson Randolph (Amazon Kindle), Kindle Location 80 percent of 100.

[405] Thomas Jefferson "Memoir" in Memoir, Correspondence, And Miscellanies, From The Papers Of Thomas Jefferson, Volume I, ed. Thomas Jefferson Randolph (Amazon Kindle), Kindle Location 17 percent of 100.

[406] Thomas Jefferson "Letter to Mann Page, 1795" in Memoir, Correspondence, And Miscellanies, From The Papers Of Thomas Jefferson, Volume III, ed. Thomas Jefferson Randolph (Amazon Kindle), Kindle Location 62 percent of 100.

[407] Thomas Jefferson "Letter to Colonel Edward Carrington, 1787" in Memoir, Correspondence, And Miscellanies, From The Papers Of Thomas Jefferson, Volume II, ed. Thomas Jefferson Randolph (Amazon Kindle), Kindle Location 18 percent of 100

[408] Ibid.

[409] Thomas Jefferson "Letter to James Madison, 1787" in Memoir, Correspondence, And Miscellanies, From The Papers Of Thomas Jefferson, Volume II, ed. Thomas Jefferson Randolph (Amazon Kindle), Kindle Location 56

"I am for preserving to the States the powers not yielded by them to the Union..."[410] – Thomas Jefferson

"Our country is too large to have all its affairs directed by a single government. Public servants at such a distance, and from under the eye of their constituents, must, from the circumstance of distance, be unable to administer and overlook all the details necessary for the good government of the citizens, and the same circumstance, by rendering detection impossible to their constituents, will invite the public agents to corruption, plunder, and waste."[411] – Thomas Jefferson

"What an augmentation of the field for jobbing, speculating, plundering, office-building, and office-hunting Would be produced by an assumption of all the State powers into the hands of the General Government."[412] – Thomas Jefferson

"I have a right to nothing, which another has a right to take away..."[413] – Thomas Jefferson

"...Kings are the servants, not the proprietors of the people."[414] – Thomas Jefferson

"The operations which have taken place in America lately fill me with pleasure. In the first place, they realize the confidence I had, that, whenever our affairs go obviously wrong, the good sense of the people will interpose, and set them to rights."[415] – Thomas Jefferson

"Never was there a country [France] where the practice of governing too much, had taken deeper root and done more mischief."[416] – Thomas Jefferson

"For when men meet together, they will make business, if they have none; they will collate their grievances, some real, some imaginary, all highly painted; they will communicate to each other the sparks of discontent; and these may engender a flame, which will consume their particular, as well as the general happiness."[417] – Thomas Jefferson

---

percent of 100.

[410] Thomas Jefferson "Letter to Elbridge Gerry, 1799" in Memoir, Correspondence, And Miscellanies, From The Papers Of Thomas Jefferson, Volume III, ed. Thomas Jefferson Randolph (Amazon Kindle), Kindle Location 80 percent of 100.

[411] Thomas Jefferson "Letter to Gideon Granger, 1800" in Memoir, Correspondence, And Miscellanies, From The Papers Of Thomas Jefferson, Volume III, ed. Thomas Jefferson Randolph (Amazon Kindle), Kindle Location 85 percent of 100.

[412] Ibid.

[413] Thomas Jefferson "Letter to James Madison, 1787" in Memoir, Correspondence, And Miscellanies, From The Papers Of Thomas Jefferson, Volume II, ed. Thomas Jefferson Randolph (Amazon Kindle), Kindle Location 56 percent of 100.

[414] Thomas Jefferson "Appendix to the Memoir, Instructions to the first Delegation" in Memoir, Correspondence, And Miscellanies, From The Papers Of Thomas Jefferson, Volume I, ed. Thomas Jefferson Randolph (Amazon Kindle), Kindle Location 28 percent of 100.

[415] Thomas Jefferson "Letter to Colonel Humphreys, 1789" in Memoir, Correspondence, And Miscellanies, From The Papers Of Thomas Jefferson, Volume II, ed. Thomas Jefferson Randolph (Amazon Kindle), Kindle Location 91 percent of 100.

[416] Thomas Jefferson "Letter to James Madison, 1789" in Memoir, Correspondence, And Miscellanies, From The Papers Of Thomas Jefferson, Volume III, ed. Thomas Jefferson Randolph (Amazon Kindle), Kindle Location 7 percent of 100.

"What a stupendous, what an incomprehensible machine is man! [W]ho can endure toil, famine, stripes, imprisonment, and death itself, in vindication of his own liberty, and, the next moment, be deaf to all those motives whose power supported him through his trial, and inflict on his fellow men a bondage, one hour of which is fraught with more misery, than ages of that which he rose in rebellion to oppose! But we must await, with patience, the workings of an overruling Providence, and hope that that is preparing the deliverance of these our suffering brethren."[418] – Thomas Jefferson

"I went, therefore, daily from Paris to Versailles, and attended their debates, generally till the hour of adjournment. Those of the Noblesse were impassioned and tempestuous. They had some able men on both sides, actuated by equal zeal. The debates of the Commons were temperate, rational, and inflexibly firm."[419] – Thomas Jefferson

"...[T]hey are removed from the reach of fear, the only restraining motive which may hold the hand of a tyrant."[420] – Thomas Jefferson

"If our country, when pressed with wrongs at the point of the bayonet, had been governed by its heads instead of its' hearts, where should we have been now? Hanging on a gallows as high as Hainan's."[421] – Thomas Jefferson

"We think, in America, that it is necessary to introduce the people into every department of government, as far as they are capable of exercising it: and that this is the only way to insure a long continued and honest administration of its powers."[422] – Thomas Jefferson

"Nor will any degree of power in the hands of government prevent insurrections. In England, where the hand of power is heavier than with us, there are seldom half a dozen years without an insurrection."[423] - Thomas Jefferson

---

[417] Thomas Jefferson "Article by Jefferson: 'Estats Unis,' For the Encyclopedie Methodique" in Memoir, Correspondence, And Miscellanies, From The Papers Of Thomas Jefferson, Volume I, ed. Thomas Jefferson Randolph (Amazon Kindle), Kindle Location 92 percent of 100.

[418] Thomas Jefferson "Article by Jefferson: 'Estats Unis,' For the Encyclopedie Methodique" in Memoir, Correspondence, And Miscellanies, From The Papers Of Thomas Jefferson, Volume I, ed. Thomas Jefferson Randolph (Amazon Kindle), Kindle Location 93 percent of 100.

[419] Thomas Jefferson "Memoir" in Memoir, Correspondence, And Miscellanies, From The Papers Of Thomas Jefferson, Volume I, ed. Thomas Jefferson Randolph (Amazon Kindle), Kindle Location 19 percent of 100.

[420] Thomas Jefferson "Appendix to the Memoir, Instructions to the first Delegation" in Memoir, Correspondence, And Miscellanies, From The Papers Of Thomas Jefferson, Volume I, ed. Thomas Jefferson Randolph (Amazon Kindle), Kindle Location 26 percent of 100.

[421] Thomas Jefferson "Letter to Mrs. Cosway, 1786" in Memoir, Correspondence, And Miscellanies, From The Papers Of Thomas Jefferson, Volume II, ed. Thomas Jefferson Randolph (Amazon Kindle), Kindle Location 12 percent of 100.

[422] Thomas Jefferson "Letter to M. L'Abbe Arnond, 1789" in Memoir, Correspondence, And Miscellanies, From The Papers Of Thomas Jefferson, Volume III, ed. Thomas Jefferson Randolph (Amazon Kindle), Kindle Location 4 percent of 100.

[423] Thomas Jefferson "Letter to James Madison, 1787" in Memoir, Correspondence, And Miscellanies, From The Papers Of Thomas Jefferson, Volume II, ed. Thomas Jefferson Randolph (Amazon Kindle), Kindle Location 56 percent of 100.

"And those who have once got an ascendency, and possessed themselves of all the resources of the nation, their revenues and offices, have immense means for retaining their advantage."[424] – Thomas Jefferson

"It is a singular phenomenon, that while our State governments are the very best in the world, without exception or comparison, our General Government has, in the rapid course of nine or ten years, become more arbitrary, and has swallowed more of the public liberty, than even that of England."[425] – Thomas Jefferson

"Let us deserve well of our country by making her interests the end of all our plans, and not our own pomp, patronage, and irresponsibility."[426] – Thomas Jefferson

"With respect to the State of Virginia in particular, the people seem to have laid aside the monarchial, and taken up the republican government, with as much ease as would have attended their throwing off an old and putting on a new suit of clothes. Not a single throe has attended this important transformation. A half dozen aristocratical gentlemen, agonizing under the loss of pre-eminence, have sometimes ventured their sarcasms on our political metamorphosis. They have been thought fitter objects of pity than of punishment."[427] – Thomas Jefferson

"No race of kings has ever presented above one man of common, sense, in twenty generations. The best they can do is, to leave things to their ministers; and what are their ministers, but a committee, badly chosen?"[428] – Thomas Jefferson

"I retired much poorer than when I entered the public service, and desired nothing but rest and oblivion."[429] – Thomas Jefferson

"My great anxiety at present is, to avail ourselves of our ascendency to establish good principles, and good practices: to fortify republicanism behind as many barriers as possible, that the outworks may give time to rally and save the citadel, should that be again in danger."[430] – Thomas Jefferson

---

[424] Thomas Jefferson "Letter to John Taylor, 1798" in Memoir, Correspondence, And Miscellanies, From The Papers Of Thomas Jefferson, Volume III, ed. Thomas Jefferson Randolph (Amazon Kindle), Kindle Location 77 percent of 100.

[425] Thomas Jefferson "Letter to John Taylor, 1798" in Memoir, Correspondence, And Miscellanies, From The Papers Of Thomas Jefferson, Volume III, ed. Thomas Jefferson Randolph (Amazon Kindle), Kindle Location 79 percent of 100.

[426] Thomas Jefferson "Letter to Albert Gallatin, 1802" in Memoir, Correspondence, And Miscellanies, From The Papers Of Thomas Jefferson, Volume III, ed. Thomas Jefferson Randolph (Amazon Kindle), Kindle Location 95 percent of 100.

[427] Thomas Jefferson "Letter to Dr. Benjamin Franklin, 1777" in Memoir, Correspondence, And Miscellanies, From The Papers Of Thomas Jefferson, Volume I, ed. Thomas Jefferson Randolph (Amazon Kindle), Kindle Location 38 percent of 100.

[428] Thomas Jefferson "Letter to Mr. Hawkins, 1787" in Memoir, Correspondence, And Miscellanies, From The Papers Of Thomas Jefferson, Volume II, ed. Thomas Jefferson Randolph (Amazon Kindle), Kindle Location 43 percent of 100.

[429] Thomas Jefferson "Letter to Edward Rutledge, 1796" in Memoir, Correspondence, And Miscellanies, From The Papers Of Thomas Jefferson, Volume III, ed. Thomas Jefferson Randolph (Amazon Kindle), Kindle Location 66 percent of 100.

[430] Thomas Jefferson "Letter to John Dickinson, 1801" in Memoir, Correspondence, And Miscellanies, From The

On Labor, Ownership of Wealth and Economics:

"Agriculture, manufactures, commerce, and navigation, the four pillars of our prosperity, are then most thriving when left most free to individual enterprise."[431] – Thomas Jefferson

"I am anxious about every thing which may affect our credit. My wish would be, to possess it in the highest degree, but to use it little."[432] – Thomas Jefferson

"By suppressing at once the whole internal taxes, we abolish three fourths of the offices now existing, and spread over the land."[433] – Thomas Jefferson

"The maxim of buying nothing without the money in our pockets to pay for it, would make of our country one of the happiest upon earth."[434] – Thomas Jefferson

"These, fellow citizens, are the circumstances under which we meet, and we remark with special satisfaction those which under the smiles of Providence result from the skill, industry, and order of our citizens, managing their own affairs in their own way and for their own use, unembarrassed by too much regulation, unoppressed by fiscal exactions."[435] – Thomas Jefferson

"...[W]e might hope to see the finances of the Union as clear and intelligible as a merchant's books, so that every member of Congress, and every man of any mind in the Union, should be able to comprehend them, to investigate abuses, and consequently to control them."[436] - Thomas Jefferson

"We shall now get rid of the commissioner of the internal revenue..."[437] – Thomas Jefferson

"They, in order to increase expense, debt, taxation, and patronage, tried always how much they could give."[438] – Thomas Jefferson

---

Papers Of Thomas Jefferson, Volume III, ed. Thomas Jefferson Randolph (Amazon Kindle), Kindle Location 94 percent of 100.

[431] Thomas Jefferson "State of the Union Address, Dec. 8, 1801" in State of the Union Address, Thomas Jefferson, A Public Domain Book, (Amazon Kindle), Kindle Location 11 percent of 100.

[432] Thomas Jefferson "Letter to General Washington, 1788" in Memoir, Correspondence, And Miscellanies, From The Papers Of Thomas Jefferson, Volume II, ed. Thomas Jefferson Randolph (Amazon Kindle), Kindle Location 61 percent of 100.

[433] Thomas Jefferson "Letter to John Dickinson, 1801" in Memoir, Correspondence, And Miscellanies, From The Papers Of Thomas Jefferson, Volume III, ed. Thomas Jefferson Randolph (Amazon Kindle), Kindle Location 95 percent of 100.

[434] Thomas Jefferson "Letter to A. Donald, 1787" in Memoir, Correspondence, And Miscellanies, From The Papers Of Thomas Jefferson, Volume II, ed. Thomas Jefferson Randolph (Amazon Kindle), Kindle Location 40 percent of 100.

[435] Thomas Jefferson "State of the Union Address, Dec. 15, 1802" in State of the Union Address, Thomas Jefferson, A Public Domain Book, (Amazon Kindle), Kindle Location 15 percent of 100.

[436] Thomas Jefferson "Letter to Albert Gallatin, 1802" in Memoir, Correspondence, And Miscellanies, From The Papers Of Thomas Jefferson, Volume III, ed. Thomas Jefferson Randolph (Amazon Kindle), Kindle Location 95 percent of 100.

[437] Ibid.

[438] Thomas Jefferson "Letter to Governor Monroe, 1803" in Memoir, Correspondence, And Miscellanies, From The Papers Of Thomas Jefferson, Volume III, ed. Thomas Jefferson Randolph (Amazon Kindle), Kindle Location 97

"Have you considered all the consequences of your proposition respecting post-roads? I view it as a source of boundless patronage to the executive, jobbing to members of Congress and their friends, and a bottomless abyss of public money. You will begin by only appropriating the surplus of the post-office revenues: but the other revenues will soon be called in to their aid, and it will be a source of eternal scramble among the members, who can get the most money wasted in their state; and they will always get the most who are meanest."[439] – Thomas Jefferson

"To reform the prodigalities [wasteful expenditures] of our predecessors is understood to be peculiarly our duty, and to bring the government to a simple and economical course."[440] – Thomas Jefferson

"...[W]eighing all probabilities of expense as well as of income, there is reasonable ground of confidence that we may now safely dispense with all the internal taxes...and that the remaining sources of revenue will be sufficient to provide for the support of Government, to pay the interest of the public debts, and to discharge the principals within shorter periods than the laws or the general expectation had contemplated."[441] – Thomas Jefferson

"It is contrary to the spirit of trade, and to the dispositions of merchants, to carry a commodity to any market where but one person is allowed to buy it, and where, of course, that person fixes its price, which the seller must receive, or reexport his commodity, at the loss of his voyage thither."[442] – Thomas Jefferson

"Considering the general tendency to multiply offices and dependencies and to increase expense...it behooves us to avail ourselves of every occasion which presents itself for taking off the surcharge, that it never may be seen here that after leaving to labor [the working populace] the smallest portion of its earnings on which it can subsist, Government shall itself consume the whole residue of what it was instituted to guard."[443] – Thomas Jefferson

"But with respect to future debts, would it not be wise and just for that nation to declare in the constitution they are forming, that neither the legislature nor the nation itself, can validly contract more debt than they may pay within their own age, or within the term of thirty-four years?"[444] – Thomas Jefferson

---

percent of 100.

[439] Thomas Jefferson "Letter to James Madison, 1796" in Memoir, Correspondence, And Miscellanies, From The Papers Of Thomas Jefferson, Volume III, ed. Thomas Jefferson Randolph (Amazon Kindle), Kindle Location 63 percent of 100.

[440] Thomas Jefferson "Letter to Governor Monroe, 1803" in Memoir, Correspondence, And Miscellanies, From The Papers Of Thomas Jefferson, Volume III, ed. Thomas Jefferson Randolph (Amazon Kindle), Kindle Location 97 percent of 100.

[441] Thomas Jefferson "State of the Union Address, Dec. 8, 1801" in State of the Union Address, Thomas Jefferson, A Public Domain Book, (Amazon Kindle), Kindle Location 4 percent of 100.

[442] Thomas Jefferson "Letter to The Count De Vergennes, 1785" in Memoir, Correspondence, And Miscellanies, From The Papers Of Thomas Jefferson, Volume I, ed. Thomas Jefferson Randolph (Amazon Kindle), Kindle Location 63 percent of 100.

[443] Thomas Jefferson "State of the Union Address, Dec. 8, 1801" in State of the Union Address, Thomas Jefferson, A Public Domain Book, (Amazon Kindle), Kindle Location 6 percent of 100.

[444] Thomas Jefferson "Letter to James Madison, 1789" in Memoir, Correspondence, And Miscellanies, From The Papers Of Thomas Jefferson, Volume III, ed. Thomas Jefferson Randolph (Amazon Kindle), Kindle Location 8

"When effects so salutary result from the plans you have already sanctioned; when merely by avoiding false objects of expense we are able, without a direct tax, without internal taxes, and without borrowing to make large and effectual payments toward the discharge of our public debt and the emancipation of our posterity from that mortal canker, it is an encouragement, fellow citizens, of the highest order to proceed as we have begun in substituting economy for taxation..."[445] –Thomas Jefferson

"The conclusion, then, is, that neither the representatives of a nation, nor the whole nation itself assembled, can validly engage debts beyond what they may pay in their own time..."[446] – Thomas Jefferson

"The accounts of the United States ought to be, and may be, made as simple as those of a common farmer..."[447] – Thomas Jefferson

"I wish to Heaven that our new government may see the importance of putting themselves immediately into a respectable position. To make provision for the speedy payment of their foreign debts, will be the first operation necessary."[448] – Thomas Jefferson

"In the mean time, by payments of the principal of our debt, we are liberating annually portions of the external taxes and forming from them a growing fund still further to lessen the necessity of recurring to extraordinary resources."[449] – Thomas Jefferson

"I wish it were possible to obtain a single amendment to our constitution. I would be willing to depend on that alone for the reduction of the administration of our government to the genuine principles of its constitution; I mean an additional article, taking from the federal government the power of borrowing."[450] – Thomas Jefferson

"I look back to the time of the war, as a time of happiness and enjoyment, when amidst the privation of many things not essential to happiness, we could not run in debt, because nobody would trust us; when we practiced, of necessity, the maxim of buying nothing but what we had money in our pockets to pay for; a maxim, which, of all others, lays the broadest foundation for happiness."[451] – Thomas Jefferson

---

percent of 100.

[445] Thomas Jefferson "State of the Union Address, Dec. 15, 1802" in State of the Union Address, Thomas Jefferson, A Public Domain Book, (Amazon Kindle), Kindle Location 21 percent of 100.

[446] Thomas Jefferson "Letter to James Madison, 1789" in Memoir, Correspondence, And Miscellanies, From The Papers Of Thomas Jefferson, Volume III, ed. Thomas Jefferson Randolph (Amazon Kindle), Kindle Location 8 percent of 100.

[447] Thomas Jefferson "Letter to James Madison, 1796" in Memoir, Correspondence, And Miscellanies, From The Papers Of Thomas Jefferson, Volume III, ed. Thomas Jefferson Randolph (Amazon Kindle), Kindle Location 63 percent of 100.

[448] Thomas Jefferson "Letter to John Brown, 1788" in Memoir, Correspondence, And Miscellanies, From The Papers Of Thomas Jefferson, Volume II, ed. Thomas Jefferson Randolph (Amazon Kindle), Kindle Location 64 percent of 100.

[449] Thomas Jefferson "State of the Union Address, Dec. 15, 1802" in State of the Union Address, Thomas Jefferson, A Public Domain Book, (Amazon Kindle), Kindle Location 21 percent of 100.

[450] Thomas Jefferson "Letter to John Taylor, 1798" in Memoir, Correspondence, And Miscellanies, From The Papers Of Thomas Jefferson, Volume III, ed. Thomas Jefferson Randolph (Amazon Kindle), Kindle Location 79 percent of 100.

"We consider it as of the first importance, to possess the first credit...and to use it little."[452] – Thomas Jefferson

"On the 12th, I obtained leave to bring in a bill declaring tenants in tail to hold their lands in fee simple. In the earlier times of the colony, where lands were to be obtained for little or nothing, some provident individuals procured large grants; and, desirous of founding great families for themselves, settled them on their descendants in fee tail. The transmission of this property from generation to generation, in the same name, raised up a distinct set of families, who, being privileged...were thus formed into a Patrician order, distinguished by the splendor and luxury of their establishments....To annul this privilege and...make an opening for the aristocracy of virtue and talent...no violence was necessary, no deprivation of natural right, but rather an enlargement of it by a repeal of the law. For this would authorize the present holder to divide the property among his children equally, as his affections were divided; and would place them, by natural generation, on the level of their fellow citizens."[453] – Thomas Jefferson

On Judicial Activism and Overreach:

"They [federal judges] are then, in fact, the corps of sappers and miners, steadily working to undermine the independent rights of the states, and to consolidate all power in the hands of that [federal] government, in which they have so important a freehold estate."[454] – Thomas Jefferson

"To this bias add that of the *esprit de corps*, of their [judges] peculiar maxim and creed, that 'it is the office of a good Judge to enlarge his jurisdiction,' and the absence of responsibility; and how can we expect impartial decision between the General government, of which they are themselves so eminent a part, and an individual state, from which they have nothing to hope or fear?"[455] – Thomas Jefferson

"We have seen, too, that, contrary to all correct example, they [judges] are in the habit of going out of the question before them, to throw an anchor ahead, and grapple further hold for future advances of power."[456] – Thomas Jefferson

"As, for the safety of society, we commit honest maniacs to Bedlam, so judges should be withdrawn from their bench, whose erroneous biases are leading us to dissolution."[457] – Thomas Jefferson

---

[451] Thomas Jefferson "Letter to Mr. Skipwith, 1787" in Memoir, Correspondence, And Miscellanies, From The Papers Of Thomas Jefferson, Volume II, ed. Thomas Jefferson Randolph (Amazon Kindle), Kindle Location 39 percent of 100.

[452] Thomas Jefferson "Letter to Mr. Dumas, 1790" in Memoir, Correspondence, And Miscellanies, From The Papers Of Thomas Jefferson, Volume III, ed. Thomas Jefferson Randolph (Amazon Kindle), Kindle Location 14 percent of 100.

[453] Thomas Jefferson "Memoir" in Memoir, Correspondence, And Miscellanies, From The Papers Of Thomas Jefferson, Volume I, ed. Thomas Jefferson Randolph (Amazon Kindle), Kindle Location 9 percent of 100.

[454] Thomas Jefferson "Memoir" in Memoir, Correspondence, And Miscellanies, From The Papers Of Thomas Jefferson, Volume I, ed. Thomas Jefferson Randolph (Amazon Kindle), Kindle Location 17 percent of 100.

[455] Ibid.

[456] Ibid.

[457] Ibid.

"It is in the power, therefore, of the juries, if they think the permanent judges are under any bias whatever, in any cause, to take on themselves to judge the law as well as the fact."[458] – Thomas Jefferson

"By a fraudulent use of the constitution, which has made judges irremovable, they have multiplied useless judges merely to strengthen their phalanx."[459] – Thomas Jefferson

"On their part, they have retired into the judiciary as a strong hold. There the remains of federalism are to be preserved and fed from the treasury, and from that battery all the works of republicanism are to be beaten down and erased."[460] – Thomas Jefferson

Religion, Morals, Civil Society and Their Effect on Government:

"When we assemble together, fellow citizens, to consider the state of our beloved country, our just attentions are first drawn to those pleasing circumstances which mark the goodness of that Being from whose favor they flow and the large measure of thankfulness we owe for His bounty. Another year has come around, and finds us still blessed with peace and friendship abroad; law, order, and religion at home..."[461] – Thomas Jefferson

"To give greater emphasis to our proposition, we agreed to wait the next morning on Mr. Nicholas, whose grave and religious character was more in unison with the tone of our resolution, and to solicit him to move it."[462] – Thomas Jefferson

"[T]he Christian religion...is a religion of all others most friendly to liberty, science, and the freest expansion of the human mind."[463] – Thomas Jefferson

"We hold these truths to be self evident: that all men are created equal; that they are endowed by their creator with...inalienable rights..."[464] – Thomas Jefferson

"...[We] put our existence to the hazard, when the hazard seemed against us, and we saved our country: justifying, at the same time, the ways of Providence, whose precept is, to do always what is right, and leave the issue to him."[465] – Thomas Jefferson

---

[458] Thomas Jefferson "Letter to M. L'Abbe Arnond, 1789" in Memoir, Correspondence, And Miscellanies, From The Papers Of Thomas Jefferson, Volume III, ed. Thomas Jefferson Randolph (Amazon Kindle), Kindle Location 4 percent of 100.

[459] Thomas Jefferson "Letter to John Dickinson, 1801" in Memoir, Correspondence, And Miscellanies, From The Papers Of Thomas Jefferson, Volume III, ed. Thomas Jefferson Randolph (Amazon Kindle), Kindle Location 94 percent of 100.

[460] Ibid.

[461] Thomas Jefferson "State of the Union Address, Dec. 15, 1802" in State of the Union Address, Thomas Jefferson, A Public Domain Book, (Amazon Kindle), Kindle Location 15 percent of 100.

[462] Thomas Jefferson "Memoir" in Memoir, Correspondence, And Miscellanies, From The Papers Of Thomas Jefferson, Volume I, ed. Thomas Jefferson Randolph (Amazon Kindle), Kindle Location 4 percent of 100.

[463] Thomas Jefferson "Letter to Moses Robinson, 1801" in Memoir, Correspondence, And Miscellanies, From The Papers Of Thomas Jefferson, Volume III, ed. Thomas Jefferson Randolph (Amazon Kindle), Kindle Location 90 percent of 100.

[464] Thomas Jefferson "Memoir, A Declaration by the Representatives of the United States of America, in General Congress Assembled" in Memoir, Correspondence, And Miscellanies, From The Papers Of Thomas Jefferson, Volume I, ed. Thomas Jefferson Randolph (Amazon Kindle), Kindle Location 6 percent of 100.

[465] Thomas Jefferson "Letter to Mrs. Cosway, 1786" in Memoir, Correspondence, And Miscellanies, From The Papers Of Thomas Jefferson, Volume II, ed. Thomas Jefferson Randolph (Amazon Kindle), Kindle Location 12

"The God who gave us life, gave us liberty at the same time: the hand of force may destroy, but cannot disjoin them."[466] – Thomas Jefferson

"Give up money, give up fame, give up science, give the earth itself and all it contains, rather than do an immoral act."[467] – Thomas Jefferson

"Conjugal love having no existence among them, domestic happiness, of which that is the basis, is utterly unknown."[468] – Thomas Jefferson

"If ever you find yourself environed with difficulties and perplexing circumstances, out of which you are at a loss how to extricate yourself, do what is right and be assured that that will extricate you the best out of the worst situations."[469] – Thomas Jefferson

"Whenever you are to do a thing, though it can never be known but to yourself, ask yourself how you would act were all the world looking at you, and act accordingly."[470] – Thomas Jefferson

"And never suppose, that in any possible situation, or under any circumstances, it is best for you to do a dishonorable thing, however slightly so it may appear to you."[471] – Thomas Jefferson

"Encourage all your virtuous dispositions, and exercise them whenever an opportunity arises; being assured that they will gain strength by exercise, as limb of the body does, and that exercise will make them habitual."[472] – Thomas Jefferson

"Morals were too essential to the happiness of man, to be risked on the uncertain combinations of the head."[473] – Thomas Jefferson

"Wealth, title, office, are no recommendations to my friendship."[474] – Thomas Jefferson

On Private Gun Ownership:

---

percent of 100.

466 Thomas Jefferson "Appendix to the Memoir, Instructions to the first Delegation" in Memoir, Correspondence, And Miscellanies, From The Papers Of Thomas Jefferson, Volume I, ed. Thomas Jefferson Randolph (Amazon Kindle), Kindle Location 28 percent of 100.

467 Thomas Jefferson "Letter to Peter Carr – Advice to a young man, 1785" in Memoir, Correspondence, And Miscellanies, From The Papers Of Thomas Jefferson, Volume I, ed. Thomas Jefferson Randolph (Amazon Kindle), Kindle Location 64 percent of 100.

468 Thomas Jefferson "Letter to Mr. Bellini, 1785" in Memoir, Correspondence, And Miscellanies, From The Papers Of Thomas Jefferson, Volume I, ed. Thomas Jefferson Randolph (Amazon Kindle), Kindle Location 72 percent of 100.

469 Thomas Jefferson "Letter to Peter Carr – Advice to a young man, 1785" in Memoir, Correspondence, And Miscellanies, From The Papers Of Thomas Jefferson, Volume I, ed. Thomas Jefferson Randolph (Amazon Kindle), Kindle Location 64 percent of 100..

470 Ibid.

471 Ibid.

472 Ibid.

473 Thomas Jefferson "Letter to Mrs. Cosway, 1786" in Memoir, Correspondence, And Miscellanies, From The Papers Of Thomas Jefferson, Volume II, ed. Thomas Jefferson Randolph (Amazon Kindle), Kindle Location 12 percent of 100.

474 Ibid.

"Though I do not know that it will ever be of the least importance to me, yet one loves to possess arms, though they hope never to have occasion for them."[475] – Thomas Jefferson

"Let your gun therefore be the constant companion of your walks."[476] – Thomas Jefferson

"Our citizens have been always free to make, vend, and export arms. It is the constant occupation and livelihood of some of them."[477] – Thomas Jefferson

"As to the species of exercise, I advise the gun. While this gives a moderate exercise to the body, it gives boldness, enterprise, and independence to the mind."[478] – Thomas Jefferson

On Patriotism:

"So, ask the traveled inhabitant of any nation, In what country on earth would you rather live? – Certainly, in my own, where are all my friends, my relations, and the earliest and sweetest affections and recollections of my life."[479] – Thomas Jefferson

"The first object of my heart is my own country. In that is embarked my family, my fortune, and my own existence."[480] – Thomas Jefferson

"Wretched, indeed, is the nation, in whose affairs foreign powers are once permitted to intermeddle."[481] – Thomas Jefferson

On National Defense:

"Justice indeed, on our part, will save us from those wars which would have been produced by a contrary disposition. But how can we prevent those produced by the wrongs of other nations? By putting ourselves in a condition to punish them. Weakness provokes insult and injury, while a condition to punish, often prevents them."[482] – Thomas Jefferson

---

[475] Thomas Jefferson "Letter to The President, 1796" in Memoir, Correspondence, And Miscellanies, From The Papers Of Thomas Jefferson, Volume III, ed. Thomas Jefferson Randolph (Amazon Kindle), Kindle Location 65 percent of 100.

[476] Thomas Jefferson "Letter to Peter Carr – Advice to a young man, 1785" in Memoir, Correspondence, And Miscellanies, From The Papers Of Thomas Jefferson, Volume I, ed. Thomas Jefferson Randolph (Amazon Kindle), Kindle Location 64 percent of 100.

[477] Thomas Jefferson "Letter to Mr. Hammond, 1793" in Memoir, Correspondence, And Miscellanies, From The Papers Of Thomas Jefferson, Volume III, ed. Thomas Jefferson Randolph (Amazon Kindle), Kindle Location 46 percent of 100.

[478] Thomas Jefferson "Letter to Peter Carr – Advice to a young man, 1785" in Memoir, Correspondence, And Miscellanies, From The Papers Of Thomas Jefferson, Volume I, ed. Thomas Jefferson Randolph (Amazon Kindle), Kindle Location 64 percent of 100.

[479] Thomas Jefferson "Memoir" in Memoir, Correspondence, And Miscellanies, From The Papers Of Thomas Jefferson, Volume I, ed. Thomas Jefferson Randolph (Amazon Kindle), Kindle Location 22 percent of 100.

[480] Thomas Jefferson "Letter to Elbridge Gerry, 1799" in Memoir, Correspondence, And Miscellanies, From The Papers Of Thomas Jefferson, Volume III, ed. Thomas Jefferson Randolph (Amazon Kindle), Kindle Location 80 percent of 100.

[481] Thomas Jefferson "Letter to B. Vaughan, 1787" in Memoir, Correspondence, And Miscellanies, From The Papers Of Thomas Jefferson, Volume II, ed. Thomas Jefferson Randolph (Amazon Kindle), Kindle Location 37 percent of 100.

[482] Thomas Jefferson "Letter to John Jay, 1785" in Memoir, Correspondence, And Miscellanies, From The Papers Of Thomas Jefferson, Volume I, ed. Thomas Jefferson Randolph (Amazon Kindle), Kindle Location 65 percent of 100.

"I think it to our interest to punish the first insult: because an insult unpunished is the parent of many others."[483] – Thomas Jefferson

"We are, therefore, never safe till our magazines are filled with arms. The present season of truce, or peace, should, in my opinion, be improved without a moment's respite, to effect this essential object, and no means be omitted, by which money may be obtained for the purpose."[484] – Thomas Jefferson

"The power of making war often prevents it, and in our case, would give efficacy to our desire of peace."[485] – Thomas Jefferson

"For by nature's law, man is at peace with man till some aggression is committed, which, by the same law, authorizes one to destroy another as his enemy."[486] – Thomas Jefferson

"Peace and friendship with all mankind is our wisest policy: and I wish we may be permitted to pursue it. But the temper and folly of our enemies may not leave this in our choice."[487] – Thomas Jefferson

"The continuance of this peace will depend on their idea of our power to enforce it..."[488] – Thomas Jefferson

"It is our duty still to endeavor to avoid war: but if it shall actually take place, no matter by whom brought on, we must defend ourselves. If our house be on fire, without inquiring whether it was fired from within or without, we must try to extinguish it."[489] – Thomas Jefferson

"Our citizens are entitled to effectual protection..."[490] – Thomas Jefferson

"The day is within my time as well as yours, when we may say by what laws other nations shall treat us on the sea. And we will say it."[491] – Thomas Jefferson

---

[483] Ibid.

[484] Thomas Jefferson "Letter to John Jay, 1787" in Memoir, Correspondence, And Miscellanies, From The Papers Of Thomas Jefferson, Volume II, ed. Thomas Jefferson Randolph (Amazon Kindle), Kindle Location 53 percent of 100.

[485] Thomas Jefferson "Letter to General Washington, 1788" in Memoir, Correspondence, And Miscellanies, From The Papers Of Thomas Jefferson, Volume II, ed. Thomas Jefferson Randolph (Amazon Kindle), Kindle Location 82 percent of 100.

[486] Thomas Jefferson "Letter to Mr. Genet, 1793" in Memoir, Correspondence, And Miscellanies, From The Papers Of Thomas Jefferson, Volume III, ed. Thomas Jefferson Randolph (Amazon Kindle), Kindle Location 50 percent of 100.

[487] Thomas Jefferson "Letter to Mr. Dumas, 1789" in Memoir, Correspondence, And Miscellanies, From The Papers Of Thomas Jefferson, Volume II, ed. Thomas Jefferson Randolph (Amazon Kindle), Kindle Location 4 percent of 100.

[488] Thomas Jefferson "Letter to Colonel Monroe, 1786" in Memoir, Correspondence, And Miscellanies, From The Papers Of Thomas Jefferson, Volume II, ed. Thomas Jefferson Randolph (Amazon Kindle), Kindle Location 6 percent of 100.

[489] Thomas Jefferson "Letter to James Lewis, Junior, 1798" in Memoir, Correspondence, And Miscellanies, From The Papers Of Thomas Jefferson, Volume III, ed. Thomas Jefferson Randolph (Amazon Kindle), Kindle Location 76 percent of 100.

[490] Thomas Jefferson "Letter to Messrs. Carmichael and Short, 1793" in Memoir, Correspondence, And Miscellanies, From The Papers Of Thomas Jefferson, Volume III, ed. Thomas Jefferson Randolph (Amazon Kindle), Kindle Location 47 percent of 100.

[491] Thomas Jefferson "Letter to William Short, 1801" in Memoir, Correspondence, And Miscellanies, From The

"We confide in our own strength, without boasting of it; we respect that of others, without fearing it."[492] – Thomas Jefferson

"I hope our land office will rid us of our debts, and that our first attention then will be, to the beginning a naval force, of some sort."[493] – Thomas Jefferson

"I wish to Heaven that our new government may see the importance of putting themselves immediately into a respectable position. To make provision for the speedy payment of their foreign debts, will be the first operation necessary. This will give them credit. A concomitant one should be, magazines and manufactures of arms."[494] – Thomas Jefferson

"...it is proper and necessary, that we should establish a small marine force..."[495] – Thomas Jefferson

On Minority Rights:

"Does it violate [the] equal rights [of the minority] to assert some rights in the majority also? Is it political intolerance to claim a proportionate share in the direction of the public affairs? Can they not harmonize in society unless they have every thing in their own hands?"[496] – Thomas Jefferson

On American Exceptionalism:

"...[H]ow little do my countrymen know what precious blessings they are in possession of, and which no other people on earth enjoy. I confess I had no idea of it myself."[497] – Thomas Jefferson

On Party Politics:

"If I could not go to heaven but with a party, I would not go there at all."[498] – Thomas Jefferson

---

Papers Of Thomas Jefferson, Volume III, ed. Thomas Jefferson Randolph (Amazon Kindle), Kindle Location 94 percent of 100.

[492] Thomas Jefferson "Letter to Messrs. Carmichael and Short, 1793" in Memoir, Correspondence, And Miscellanies, From The Papers Of Thomas Jefferson, Volume III, ed. Thomas Jefferson Randolph (Amazon Kindle), Kindle Location 51 percent of 100.

[493] Thomas Jefferson "Letter to John Jay, 1785" in Memoir, Correspondence, And Miscellanies, From The Papers Of Thomas Jefferson, Volume I, ed. Thomas Jefferson Randolph (Amazon Kindle), Kindle Location 65 percent of 100.

[494] Thomas Jefferson "Letter to John Brown, 1788" in Memoir, Correspondence, And Miscellanies, From The Papers Of Thomas Jefferson, Volume II, ed. Thomas Jefferson Randolph (Amazon Kindle), Kindle Location 64 percent of 100.

[495] Thomas Jefferson "Letter John Adams, 1786" in Memoir, Correspondence, And Miscellanies, From The Papers Of Thomas Jefferson, Volume II, ed. Thomas Jefferson Randolph (Amazon Kindle), Kindle Location 9 percent of 100.

[496] Thomas Jefferson "Letter to a Committee of Merchants, 1801" in Memoir, Correspondence, And Miscellanies, From The Papers Of Thomas Jefferson, Volume III, ed. Thomas Jefferson Randolph (Amazon Kindle), Kindle Location 92 percent of 100.

[497] Thomas Jefferson "Letter to Colonel Monroe, 1785" in Memoir, Correspondence, And Miscellanies, From The Papers Of Thomas Jefferson, Volume I, ed. Thomas Jefferson Randolph (Amazon Kindle), Kindle Location 55 percent of 100.

[498] Thomas Jefferson "Letter to F. Hopkinson, 1789" in Memoir, Correspondence, And Miscellanies, From The Papers Of Thomas Jefferson, Volume II, ed. Thomas Jefferson Randolph (Amazon Kindle), Kindle Location 89 percent of 100.

On Crime:

"Let the legislators be merciful, but the executors of the law inexorable."[499] - Thomas Jefferson

On Slavery:

"I brought in a bill to prevent their [slaves] further importation. This passed without opposition, and stopped the increase of the evil by importation, leaving to future efforts its final eradication."[500] – Thomas Jefferson

"I am very sensible of the honor you propose to me, of becoming a member of the society for the abolition of the slave-trade."[501] – Thomas Jefferson

---

[499] Thomas Jefferson "Article by Jefferson: 'Estats Unis,' For the Encyclopedie Methodique" in Memoir, Correspondence, And Miscellanies, From The Papers Of Thomas Jefferson, Volume I, ed. Thomas Jefferson Randolph (Amazon Kindle), Kindle Location 90 percent of 100.

[500] Thomas Jefferson "Memoir" in Memoir, Correspondence, And Miscellanies, From The Papers Of Thomas Jefferson, Volume I, ed. Thomas Jefferson Randolph (Amazon Kindle), Kindle Location 9 percent of 100.

[501] Thomas Jefferson "Letter to M. Warville, 1788" in Memoir, Correspondence, And Miscellanies, From The Papers Of Thomas Jefferson, Volume II, ed. Thomas Jefferson Randolph (Amazon Kindle), Kindle Location 59 percent of 100.

Works Cited

Adams, John and Abigail. Familiar Letters of John Adams and His Wife Abigail Adams During the Revolution. New York: Hurd and Houghton, 1876. Read on Amazon Kindle.

Adams, John. State of the Union Address. Read on Amazon Kindle

Adams, John. Works of John Adams. The Perfect Library. Read on Amazon Kindle.

Adams, Samuel. The Writings of Samuel Adams - Volume 2. Collected and Edited Harry Alonso Cushing. Text prepared by Regina Azucena and Bill Stoddard. Read on Amazon Kindle.

Adams, Samuel. The Writings of Samuel Adams - Volume 3. Collected and Edited Harry Alonso Cushing. Text prepared by Regina Azucena and Daniel Moore. Read on Amazon Kindle.

Adams, Samuel. The Writings of Samuel Adams - Volume 4. Collected and Edited Harry Alonso Cushing. Read on Amazon Kindle.

Brands, H.W. The First American, The Life and Times of Benjamin Franklin. New York: Doubleday, 2000. Print.

Coulter, Ann. Treason; Liberal Treachery From The Cold War to the War on Terrorism. New York: Crown Forum, 2003. Print.

Franklin, Benjamin. Poor Richard's Almanac. United States of America: Seven Treasures Publications, 2008. Electronic. Read on Amazon Kindle.

Jefferson, Thomas. Memoir, Correspondence, and Miscellanies, From The Papers Of Thomas Jefferson, Volume 1. Ed. Thomas Jefferson Randolph. Cambridge: E.W. Metcalf & Company, 1829. Read on Amazon Kindle.

Jefferson, Thomas. Memoir, Correspondence, and Miscellanies, From The Papers Of Thomas Jefferson, Volume 2. Ed. Thomas Jefferson Randolph. Cambridge: E.W. Metcalf & Company, 1829. Read on Amazon Kindle.

Jefferson, Thomas. Memoir, Correspondence, and Miscellanies, From The Papers Of Thomas Jefferson, Volume 3. Ed. Thomas Jefferson Randolph. Cambridge: E.W. Metcalf & Company, 1829. Read on Amazon Kindle.

Jefferson, Thomas. State of the Union Address. Read on Amazon Kindle.

Lock, John. Second Treatise of Government. Digitized by Dave Gowan. England: 1690.[502] Electronic. Read on Amazon Kindle.

McCullough, David. John Adams. New York: Simon & Schuster, 2001. Print.

Paine, Thomas. Common Sense. United States: Barnes and Nobles, 1995.

Rush, Benjamin. The Selected Writings of Benjamin Rush. Ed. Dagobert D. Runes. All pages read to research this book.

Toqueville, Alexis de. Democracy in America Volume I. Boston, Massachusetts, United States of America: IndyPublish.com, 2003.

Washington, George. "Farewell Address." *The American Republic Primary Sources*. Ed. Bruce Frohnen. Indianapolis, Indiana: Liberty Fund, Inc., 2002. pp. 72-78. Print.

Washington, George. "Letter to the Roman Catholics in the United States of America." *The American Republic Primary Sources*. Ed. Bruce Frohnen. Indianapolis, Indiana: Liberty Fund, Inc., 2002. pp. 70-71. Print.

Washington, George. State of the Union Address. Read on Amazon Kindle.

Washington, George. "Thanksgiving Proclamation." *The American Republic Primary Sources*. Ed. Bruce Frohnen. Indianapolis, Indiana: Liberty Fund, Inc., 2002. pp. 69-70. Print.

[502] The original publisher put 1690 as the publication date, but the actual publication date was in December 1689.

Made in United States
Troutdale, OR
08/09/2024